99 Theses on the Revaluation of Value

Other Books by Brian Massumi
Published by the University of Minnesota Press

Architectures of the Unforeseen: Essays in the Occurrent Arts

Thought in the Act: Passages in the Ecology of Experience
ERIN MANNING AND BRIAN MASSUMI

The Politics of Everyday Fear
BRIAN MASSUMI, EDITOR

99 Theses on the Revaluation of Value

A Postcapitalist Manifesto

Brian Massumi

University of Minnesota Press

Minneapolis

London

Published by the University of Minnesota Press
111 Third Avenue South, Suite 290
Minneapolis, MN 55401-2520
http://www.upress.umn.edu

ISBN 978-1-5179-0588-0 (hc)
ISBN 978-1-5179-0587-3 (pb)

A Cataloging-in-Publication record for this book is available from the Library of Congress.

Printed in the United States of America on acid-free paper

The University of Minnesota is an equal-opportunity educator and employer.

23 22 21 20 19 18   9 8 7 6 5 4 3 2 1

Contents

99 Theses on the Revaluation of Value

A Postcapitalist Manifesto

T1

It is time to take back value. For many, value has long been dismissed as a concept so thoroughly compromised, so soaked in normative strictures and stained by complicity with capitalist power, as to be unredeemable. This has only abandoned value to purveyors of normativity and apologists of economic oppression. *Value is too valuable to be left in those hands.*

T2

In the absence of a strong *alternative conception of value,* it is all too easy for normative gestures to slip back in. Priorities are still weighed, orientations favored, directions followed. Without a concept of value, by what standards are these choices made? Usually none that are enunciated. Standards of judgment are simply allowed to operate implicitly. Normativity is not avoided. It becomes a sneak. This can prove to be just as oppressive.

T3

To take back value is *not to reimpose standards* of judgment providing a normative yardstick. That would do little other than to make the oppressiveness explicit again.

T4

To take back value is to revalue value, *beyond normativity* and standard judgment. More radically, it is to move beyond the reign of judgment itself.

T5

The first task of the revaluation of value is to *uncouple value from quantification*. Value must be recognized for what it is: irreducibly qualitative.

T6

The revaluation of value as *irreducibly qualitative* must be insistently *this-worldly*. Appealing to transcendent values, styled as moral qualities, only raises the strictures of normativity to the absolute.

> **Lemma a.** The revaluation of value is *ethical by definition.* That is why it cannot be moral.

> **SCHOLIUM.** In an ethics, the transcendent moral *opposition* (Good/Evil) and its attenuated democratic offspring (normal/pathological) are "supplanted by the qualitative *difference* of modes of existence" (Deleuze 1988, 23). Ethics bears on what, qualitatively, a process can do, and in what direction that capacitation leads. It evaluates the singular *how* of "an immanent power's" (25) mode of operation, as it consequentially unfolds. The project of a revaluation of values to give value its qualitative due takes the path of a *processual* ethics. Processual ethics is thoroughly relational. The immanently self-powering modes of existence it concerns come in multiples and mutually inflect. This qualifies it as an ecology, in the broadest sense.

Lemma b. The revaluation of values overspills the narrowly economic domain, into an *ecology of powers* (T49–T68).

T7

To uncouple value from quantification in a way that affirms an ecology of qualitatively different powers means engaging head-on with the economic logic of the market. *Value is too valuable to be left to capital.*

T8

The dominant notion of value in our epoch is economic. The domain of economic value is conceived of as the market. Market-based thinking deploys a consensus *definition of money.* That definition is threefold: unit of account, medium of exchange, and store of value.

> SCHOLIUM. This definition actually skirts the issue of value. Since the "store of value" is nothing other than a quantity of units of account held in reserve, poised to enter exchange, the definition is circular. The circularity spreads the quantitative notion of value across the three roles, equating value with the ability of money to phase between them. The result is an obfuscation of value, both of how it actually functions in capitalism— which cannot be reduced to classical market mechanisms and the market's central concept of exchange—and of what it might become in a revalued postcapitalist future.

T9

The threefold market definition of money assumes that value is by nature quantifiable and posits *money as the measure of value.* These assumptions must be questioned in order to open the way to the revaluation of value.

T10

The classical concept of the market assumes not only the quantifiability of value but the *myth of equal exchange,* as judged by the measure of money. This is the idea that one can get "value for money," guaranteeing fair exchange. This fairness principle is seen to be the engine of the capitalist market.

SCHOLIUM A. The ideas of equal exchange and getting value for money are supported by the notion of money as measure of value. Money can be treated as the measure of value because it is used as a *general equivalent*: a yardstick for comparison. With this yardstick, incommensurable things can be commensurated. A "fair" exchange is when the use-value of a commodity object is judged commensurate with its price. Price provides a standardized third term enabling qualitatively different commodity objects to be compared. This, in theory, enables "rational" consumer choice. The value of a present sum of money can also be compared to a sum in the future, enabling "rational" life choices. The myth of fair exchange is undermined, however, by the concurrent market logic of getting a *"good deal."* In consumer behavior, the allure of getting *more* value for your money is actually a stronger engine. This points to the fact that if you scratch the shiny surface of the market idea, the specter of *unequal exchange* immediately appears. Qualitative understandings of value then return, to shake the foundation of the quantitative vision of value. It takes little reflection to realize that the "goodness" of the good deal is only partially reflected in the price. The "calculation" of what constitutes a good deal does not only involve "rational" considerations. The sense that more value for money is obtained is strongly inflected by the subjective factors of the buyer's dispositions, desires, and idiosyncrasies. "Use-value" (T91 Schol. b) is relative, and it is impossible to separate from more subjective values such as prestige-value. These subjective factors cannot be commensurated from one consumer to another, or from one purchase to another. They are singularly qualitative "calculations." They are also object lessons in the plasticity of value.

SCHOLIUM B. The myth of the commensurability of a present sum of money and a future value is also undermined, this time by the tendency of the market itself to exemplify the plasticity of value. This is called *volatility*. Volatility is two-headed. It arises from factors endogenous to the market, such as cycles, and crises arising as complexity effects of the market's very mode of operation (speculative bubbles). It also arises from *externalities,* which include such things as wars, natural disasters, and weather (or more radically, climate change). Externalities are qualitative changes in the market's outside environment that are secondarily reflected in price changes in the market (Hardt and Negri 2009, 155). Also included are price movements linked to valuations that are not exactly outside the market but are not fundamentally "calculated" in money terms either. The classic example is the added value of location as reflected in real estate prices. Location is valued as an indicator of *quality of life.* Quality of life is not in itself measurable. Higher prices in a desirable neighborhood are a way of putting a number on the immeasurable. They numerically express an incommensurability. This suggests a connection between *value and vitality* that is reflected in pricing but is irreducible to that quantitative expression because, in itself, it is directly qualitative.

Lemma a. Actual market dynamics assume *unequal exchange.* The way the market operates in practice is predicated more on *excess* than on commensuration. More-than is more equal than equal-to.

Lemma b. The more-than unbalancing exchange is *due to qualitative factors.* Although reflected in price, these qualitative factors are and remain externalities to the market. They are of another nature than their quantitative reflection, presenting a nonnumerical excess. They remain subjective, vital: equal to qualities of experience; pertaining to quality of life.

Lemma c. A revaluation of value must contrive to develop this connection between value and vitality that is presupposed by the market but disavowed by it. It must *make qualitative excess a postcapitalist virtue*—beyond the myth of equal exchange, the fairness of the market, and the rhetoric of commensuration.

T11

The distinction between *endogenous factors and externalities* is ultimately unsustainable. This requires a rethinking of what it means for something to be *"inside"* or *"outside,"* and forces a distinction between system and process.

SCHOLIUM A. Everyone knows that fluctuations internal to the operations of the market fundamentally hinge on a certain privileged non-economic factor: *affect.* Markets run on fear and hope, confidence and insecurity. Affect is and remains an "externality," but what exactly does that mean? It cannot mean that affect is a factor that is squarely outside the scope of the economy. That would be to underestimate its constitutive force in market dynamics, and to deny the long shadow it has cast over the discipline of economics from the beginning. Did not Keynes warn his fellow economists in his then-maturing field against the "underestimation of the concealed factors of utter doubt, precariousness, hope and fear" (Keynes 1973, 122)? Concealed—or not so concealed, but officially disavowed. Affect cannot be considered to be squarely outside the market, but neither is it a formal market mechanism that is recognized as inside its system. It is not an economic operator per se. It has its own nature and modus operandi, and they are qualitative. Affect qualitatively agitates the economy, but it also overspills it, extending to many a non-economic arena. It forces itself upon economic calculations but is not one itself. Market functions feel its force. It makes its mark economically, while remaining of another nature, in excess-over. We can sum up the "subjective, vital" factors that are called "externalities" with the word "affect." Affect is a name for factors that make their mark on market dynamics while overspilling them, that modulate economic logic without belonging to it as such. A better way to capture affect's fraught status than to say that it is an externality is to say that it is the market's *immanent outside*. This term points to the fact that there are *factors that belong to capitalism's field but do not belong to its system* (Massumi 2017a, ch. 1). It is to the immanent outside of capitalism that the revaluation of values must look to identify qualitative processes in embryonic form that might grow a postcapitalist future. The question of affect is closely related to the concept of intensity (T31, T42, T43). Intensity is a key to understanding the relation between the qualitative and the quantitative in economic terms.

> **Lemma a.** The contrast just made between the economic *system* and a wider *process,* the latter pertaining to qualitative factors constituting an "immanent outside," is a necessary tool for the project of revaluing value.

SCHOLIUM B. This expands and complicates the logic of inside/outside. A system demarcates itself from other systems, and in so doing delineates its operative inside from their externality. For example, the economy is systemically defined by a certain order of operations that mutually cohere. Those operations are distinct from the operations mutually cohering in a technical system, say a steam engine. But in addition to this internal/external distinction, there is the immanent outside, as a category in its own right. The economy and the technology of the steam engine as systems are mutually *external*. But the *outside* is something else. The steam engine drove the economy in the nineteenth-century, and the economy drove the invention and proliferation of the steam engine. Each became in each other's dynamic embrace. Across their systemic difference, they are mutually included in the same, two-faced movement of becoming. The movement of double becoming is a processual coupling between two systems. The processual coupling belongs to neither system per se, but enters as formative force into the becoming of both. It constitutes their immanent outside. *Process is the immanent outside of the in-between of systems.* Since it is unbounded by any given system or set of systems, that immanent outside overspills systematicity as such. Considered in itself, this in-between is a wide-open. It is the expanded field of where systems' becoming may go, beyond where and what they are now. It is the fielding of potential. *Process is by nature in excess over system.* This means that every system a constitutively *open system.* This distinction between internal/external (*systems environment*) and immanent outside (*processual ecology*) becomes extremely important for understanding complicity and resistance under capitalism (T34 Schol. c, T60, T76 Schol. b).

    Lemma b. The *excess* that must be reclaimed and revalued for the postcapitalist future must be recognized as *processual.*

SCHOLIUM C. Close attention must be paid to the systemic operations of capitalism in all of its arenas (consumer market, labor market, and investment and the financial markets). However, systemic analysis is not enough. The analysis must extend to the expanded field of process. The word *field* is a handy way of holding on to the system/process distinction. "Capitalist field" can be used when the purview includes capitalism's immanent processual outside, with "system" reserved for the operations of the economy in the familiar restricted sense, as formalized by the traditional discipline of economics.

Lemma c. The "*capitalist process*" is how the capitalist system dips into its own immanent outside to draw out new potentials for its becoming, or continuing self-constitution.

Lemma d. The question of excess is only secondarily that of "expenditure" as connected to destruction (Bataille 1988). It more fundamentally pertains to potential, which concerns destruction only to the extent to which it positively fosters becoming.

T12

The myth of equal exchange is especially egregious as regards the *labor market*.

SCHOLIUM. The idea that salary is a fair exchange of a quantity of money for a quantity of life-time and bodily activity is identified by Marx as the foundational myth of capitalism. If this is an equal exchange, what is "profit"? Profit is an *excess* of the value the worker produces over and above the value of the money invested in his or her salary. Although the revaluation of value will also have to transcend the Marxian labor theory of value (among other reasons, because its critique is still articulated in quantitative terms, even though it points to the qualitative oppression of the "theft" of vitality; T33), this dramatically gives the lie to capitalism's assertion that its system functions on a basis of equal exchange, or value for value. Reducing the "cost of labor" is a rallying cry for those in a position to use money in another of its roles, backgrounded by its threefold market definition: money as the vehicle of investment. What is this cry to reduce labor costs, if not a heartfelt call to preserve, or widen, the inequality of the salary "exchange"? That inequality is presupposed by the vehemence of the call, even if it is disavowed in the accompanying explanatory rhetoric of "fair compensation." The antagonism between the capitalist's "fair compensation" and the worker's "fair wage" says it all. The unequal exchange of life-time and vital energies for the price of a salary demonstrates that in its investment heart-of-hearts capitalism runs as much on excess and incommensurability as it does in the market arena of consumer exchange.

T13

Excess is written into the very definition of *capital, in its difference from money* as unit of measure, medium of exchange, and store of value, and related to its role as investment money.

SCHOLIUM. Capital is defined as the potential to derive from a present quantity of money a greater quantity of money in the future. Capital is not profit. Profit is the greater quantity of money derived. Capital is the *potential* to derive that quantity. That potential is the effective *engine of the economic system.* It emergently stirs in the system's immanent processual outside.

T14

The capitalist economy, despite its calculative fervor, is more fundamentally concerned with *potential* than it is with actual quantities.

SCHOLIUM A. Potential is a qualitative concept, in that it connotes transformation. Capital, as movement of potential, is the *quality of money* as transformational force, the force driving the system's becoming. The transformation counts economically only as registered in the *statistics.* The numbers are quantitative signs of qualitative changes (changes in productivity, the changes in labor and management practices associated with increasing productivity, the life changes associated with the changes in labor and management practices, the increasing accumulation of wealth but also growing social inequality, the disruptions and opportunities of innovation, the accompanying cultural transformations, the appearance of new desires accompanying those transformations, new dispositions gelling those desires, the contingency of idiosyncrasies, sometimes going viral . . .). What the economic indexes index are life changes. They are disguised *vital signs*. Marx speaks of capital in terms of "social metabolism" and "metamorphosis." The changes that the vital signs index overspill the properly economic sphere. The potential of the economy is ultimately life potential. The question of value is a vital question. Capital has its invisible hand on the pulse of life.

SCHOLIUM B. As heterodox economic thinkers (those who reject the market fundamentalism and rational-calculation religion of classical, neoclassical, and libertarian economists) frequently remind us, money is *not a transparent instrument*. It is an operator of life relation, harvesting and distributing potential and depotentialization in processual embrace with the economy's immanent outside. The numbers assiduously count and recount the harvest and the distribution, but only indolently hint at the relation and the vital potential.

T15

The issue of excess returns, with regard to the definition of capital and its connection to potential, in the question of *surplus-value*.

SCHOLIUM. Surplus-value is another name for capital as quality of money. "Surplus"-value names capital as the ongoing potential for deriving in the future an excess-over a present quantity. This—and not equal exchange or fair value for money—is the engine of the economy.

T16

Surplus-value is primary in relation to value, as understood in terms of the market definition of money and as involving measurable quantities.

SCHOLIUM A. Surplus-value is an effect of *turnover.* It is the left-over of potential that drives the economic process forward. Profit is a punctual numerical harvest deducted from the process of surplus-value driving the economy continuously forward, across points of profit-taking. When profit is taken and used for investment, it is plowed back into the economy's driving by surplus-value. Surplus-value and profit turn over on each other, always leaving a left-over: an excess of *unabsorbed surplus-value* for the future generation of still greater profit. Surplus-value is the ever-more-than-and-again of profit.

Lemma a. Surplus-value is *immeasurable.*

SCHOLIUM B. In and of itself, surplus-value cannot be measured (Negri 1996, 151–54; Bryan and Rafferty 2013, 137, 145, 147). This is because, being always by nature in excess over any sum of profit, it is *supernumerary*, not in the sense of extra in number, but of being beyond number. This indeterminacy is mirrored in the unquantifiability of the supply of money itself, which is in constant fluctuation as the debts that constitute it are ceaselessly created and extinguished as the economic system turns over on itself (Schmitt 1980, 64–78; Ingham 2004, 142).

SCHOLIUM C. The sense in which surplus-value is associated with turnover goes beyond the usual sense of the turnover of commodities, mediated by money, or of money as it changes form. More fundamentally, the turnover at issue is the economic system in its indeterminate totality turning over on itself: rhythmically overspilling its own systematicity to dip into the processual outside in order to avail itself of the self-constituting potential to be found there. This has more to do with the unpredictability of the "mutant flows" (Schmitt 1980, 234–35) associated with the continual creation of money to make room in the system for the always-in-excess over it that is surplus-value, than it has to do with the regularity of cyclic patterns of circulation. Mutant flows are those that do not go "from known to known" but from "metamorphosis" to metamorphosis (277–78). Financial derivatives are the epitome of mutant capitalist flow (T33 Schol. d, T34 Schol. d, T46 Schol. b–c, T49 Schol. b, T50–T52).

SCHOLIUM D. The capitalist system is characterized by its relentless drive for *growth* in the service of *accumulation*. Growth and accumulation are capitalism's processual desire: its constitutive tendency (what Nietzsche might call its will to power). The surplus-value drive to excess-over gives the capitalist economy its dynamic quality of ever-moreness, for once and for all-over-again, in perpetual processual turnover. The engine of surplus-value lies at the beating heart of the capitalist system and dilates its veins. It is the expansive diastole for profit's systolic contraction. More than just the quality of money—that is how it appears inside the system, as a halo-glow around profit—surplus-value is the *processual quality of the capitalist system*. It is what gives its quantifications their dynamic quality. It is the processual subjectivity of the capitalist system, self-absorbed in the generation of the numerical objectifications that feed its formal operations. It is how capitalism dips into the expanded field of its immanent outside (diastole), no sooner to contract the movements of potential found there into its profit-making system flow (systole).

Lemma b. More properly speaking, capitalism's driving force is the *differential* between profit and surplus-value: their systemic/processual, systolic/diastolic asymmetry.

SCHOLIUM E. The concept of processual surplus-value as it is proposed here is not reducible to either absolute or relative *surplus-value as defined by Marx* (1976, 429–38). Marx's surplus-value involves exploiting a quantitative differential to harvest profit from it. Absolute surplus-value is obtained by lengthening the working day without increasing wages. Relative surplus-value is obtained by increasing productivity, so that the "socially necessary labor-time" that goes into the production of a commodity is lowered relative to a competitor's operations. Marx's definition of surplus-value hinges on the labor theory of value, according to which value is the quantity of labor-time that is "congealed" in the product (128). *Processual surplus-value,* in contradistinction to these two forms of *capitalist surplus-value,* is purely qualitative and concerns the intensity of lived potentials. It is *surplus-value of life* (T22–T23, T28–T32). Capitalist surplus-value and processual surplus-value are, of course, related, but they cannot be equated. The former is the systemic capture of the latter. Their difference—the difference between quality of activity as such and the derivation from it of a quantitative yield—is internalized by the system, to serve as its driving force. The theory of surplus-value of life, and the process-oriented revaluation of values it serves, requires a reconsideration of the labor theory of value, and a multiplication of the forms of capitalist surplus-value (T33, T34).

T17

The future-looking definition of capital understood in terms of surplus-value (the potential to generate a greater quantity of money in the future, accumulable as profit) means that capitalism is *fundamentally speculative.*

T18

The manner in which capital is speculative makes it a *power formation* in its own right.

> **SCHOLIUM A.** Capital is a *time-function.* The time element is fundamentally nonchronological, revolving around potential, which is nothing other than *futurity in the present.* It only secondarily concerns the measure of time. Primarily, it concerns time as the *qualitative interval* priming the actualization of *potential.* Speculation is not a perversion of the capitalist economy. It is of its essence. It is its power function. Capital is the economic lever of the time of potential. As such, it *captures the future* of vitality: life's qualitatively-in-the-making. It captures life potential. In this capacity, capital operates directly as a mechanism of power. Its economic functioning cannot be separated from its power function. To say that capitalism is a power over life is an understatement. It is a capture of life's in-the-making, its very becoming (it is an "ontopower"; T55). When capitalism internalizes the difference between quality and quantity and counts it as profit, it monetizes the intervals of life-time feeding its formal operations. It *economizes* life activity. It is this economization that directly constitutes a formation of power. Life activity is channeled toward modes of existence and manners of relation propitious for the generation of profit.

> **Lemma.** Power formations are *apparatuses of capture.*

> **SCHOLIUM B.** The assertion of heterodox economic thinkers that money is not just a transparent instrument of exchange but constitutes a social relation (a "claim upon society," as Simmel

put it; 1978, 176) is accurate as far as it goes, but it is not sufficient. Money is not just a social relation. It is the operator of a
power relation that is a *constitutive factor of society*—but more
than that, of *life* (T14). Money arrogates life powers to itself
(Cooper 2008).

T19

The fact that the engine of capitalism is excess (surplus-value) be-
lies the commonplace notion that price reflects *scarcity.*

> SCHOLIUM. The financial markets are where money functions
> most intensely as capital in the surplus-value sense. It is self-
> evident that in the financial markets excess is operative in a
> way that presupposes not scarcity but processual *abundance*:
> the ability to endlessly proliferate and multiply (most partic-
> ularly, in the current epoch of capital, through abstract finan-
> cial instruments such as derivatives). The operative idea is not
> "how to do with less" but how to make "always more" from
> less. The surplus-value drive is most directly expressed in the
> speculative machinations of the *financial markets,* where the
> continued surfing of the flow of surplus-value is valued more
> (excessively so) than any particular landfall in profit. Profits are
> swept in the tide of perpetual speculative motion: data points
> on the cyclic beach of wealth, no sooner deposited than swept
> away to rejoin the flow.

T20

*The financial markets offer a better point of departure for postcapi-
talist alter-economic thinking* than money in its traditional market
role as currency.

> SCHOLIUM. As already pointed out, the functioning of the
> capitalist economy cannot be explained solely with reference

to the classical market functioning of money defined in terms of equal exchange. It is in the speculative sphere of the financial markets that the processual engine of the capitalist economy shows its true processual quality (its ultimately unsustainable running after surplus-value fueling endless growth and uncurbed accumulation). Aspirationally postcapitalist alternatives must transcend the standard definition of money and the market-exchange concepts it underpins, or risk being outfoxed by capital from the get-go. They must generate notions more akin to surplus-value than to money in its threefold definition. In a sense, they have to be *more* faithful to how the capitalist process actually runs than market ideology is—the better to turn its dynamic (in the way it is said in zombie movies that dead bodies "turn," except in this case it is the inverse—a revivification). The turning of the turnover of capitalist surplus-value requires the *alter-valuing of self-driving process*. It requires the affirmation of an analogous dynamic quality of process, but one that does not lend itself to the quantification of the irreducibly qualitative that operates the economization of life.

    Lemma. Occupy surplus-value.

T21

A word for the *alter-value* that could drive a postcapitalist process is *creativity*.

    Scholium. The choice of "creativity" is made in full cognizance of the fact that neoliberal capitalism has appropriated the term. "*Innovation*" and "*creative capital*" are buzzwords signposting this capture. Surplus-value is the engine of creative advance of the capitalist system. But the quality of capital's creativity is best conveyed in a related phrase, which expresses the inherent violence of capitalism's economizaton of life's qualitatively in-the-making: "creative destruction." But what of life's in-the-making proper, considered as such, vitally instead of economically? What of the creative advance of life as it complexly plies its field of emergence, that immanent outside of the capitalist system whose qualitative differentials capitalism data mines for conversion to its own ends? Vital process too is self-driving. It too self-iterates, turning over on itself across its punctual expressions to continue apace. It too runs on excess, serially fed forward.

T22

In other words, there is a qualitative *surplus-value of life* (Massumi 2017b) that provides the fuel for capitalism's quantifications.

> **Lemma a.** Economization is the conversion of one kind of surplus-value (surplus-value of life) into another (capitalist surplus-value).

> **Lemma b.** Qualitative surplus-value of life is the processual given of the capitalist system. If it can be given to the system, perhaps it can be taken away from it. Even aside from this question of the withdrawal of surplus-value of life from quantification, it may be that it can be rejoined, *upstream of its capitalist conversion.* Even before capitalism is overcome, it may be possible to have one foot in both streams, in ways that prefigure its beyond. In that beyond, quantification would be beholden to surplus-value of life, rather than surplus-value of life being slave to accumulation.

T23

Existing alter-economic models, such as *cryptocurrencies,* are modeled on money in its market definition. However, in practice they overspill that definition, toward dynamics of surplus-value creation.

SCHOLIUM A. In the design of cryptocurrencies, an appeal is often explicitly made to the threefold definition of money. This articulation of the currency model backgrounds the increasingly obvious fact that the appeal of cryptocurrencies has been in large part their speculative dynamic. What gives them their momentum is their ability to run away with themselves, becoming veritable financial markets. They become commodities themselves (as do national currencies, in a usually more well-behaved way, on the mainstream international money market). More than mere currency, they become financial instruments, ripe for speculation: in a word, they become capital. This is clear in the history of Bitcoin, which has seen successive speculative bubbles and busts. In the avalanche of new cryptocurrencies coming in the wake of Bitcoin and beginning in earnest around 2015, the "initial coin offering" (ICO) has taken a more and more prominent role. Modeled on the initial public offering (IPO), the ICO treats cryptocurrency in analogy with stocks, in other words, as a form of equity (as capital). Equity refers to the "underlying" asset from which surplus-value and profit turnover is derived (although the very concept of an underlying asset is called into question by the way financial markets run: derivatives are defined precisely by their ability to abstract themselves from the value or even ownership of an underlying asset; T34 Schol. d). As is the case with any process of quantitative surplus-value production, this speculative dynamic fuels exploitation (Sassen 2017). With Bitcoin, those who are in a position to own the means of production (the increasingly exorbitant computing power needed to "mine" the coin) win. There is a jarring disconnect between the hypercapitalist speculative dimension of cryptocurrency and its exploitative underpinning, and the accompanying *libertarian rhetoric* of money equality for all, in independence from evil banks and "fiat" money, that has been the dominant legitimating narrative for it. The libertarian discourse deceptively brackets the entire concept of capital—practicing it to the hilt while purporting to act in the defense of the market, traditionally defined in terms of fair-value exchange, open equally to all, and fair to each (see also T89, T90).

SCHOLIUM B. There is a rapidly increasing number of emerging crypto-based alter-economy projects that attempt to design the exploitation out. Just to give two of many possible examples: *Faircoin* (https://fair.coop/faircoin/) works to counteract the libertarian cast of traditional blockchain currencies by creating a dedicated cryptocurrency for use among cooperatives that does away with the mining model and discourages speculation, in an attempt to restrict the currency as much as possible to a simple market model serving the micropayment needs of nontraditional collective economic actors. With *EnergyCoin* (under development; https://medium.com/@RafeFurst/energycoin-d08ddcab4a0c), cryptocurrency is mined by producing solar energy and feeding it into the grid. A portion of the increasing value of the coin is equally distributed among all coin holders as a kind of micro-guaranteed income, in an attempt to lessen the capitalist exploitation both of nature and of others. There are any number of ways of collectivizing cryptocurrency and attenuating its libertarian birthmark. Most, however, accept important compromises with the logic of the market. A maximally noncompromising, postblockchain speculative alter-economy is envisioned at the end of this text (T93–T98).

T24

Local currencies, for their part, strive to disable the speculative side of capital and return to the simple money model.

> SCHOLIUM. Local currencies (community-based token systems accepted by individual providers and local businesses; also known as LETs, or local exchange trading systems) embrace money in its aspect of unit of measure and medium of exchange. Some intentionally subtract the aspect of store of value through "demurrage," or negative interest on held assets, so that tokens lose value if they are hoarded. This is done to counteract the accumulation of value, which is the condition for the transformation of the currency into capital, and is always accompanied by growing inequality. Nevertheless, certain inequalities, and even class distinctions, may well creep back in. "For example, middle-class resources like tools and equipment and scarce tools and knowledge earn media of exchange credits with very little expenditure of time. Conversely, lower classes typically offer time-consuming labor-intensive services" (Ingham 2004, 185). The myth of equal exchange, which is the cornerstone of the logic of the traditional market, is retained, along with some of its contradictions, but within a generally communitarian ethos.

T25

Sharing economies also try to disenable economic speculation—and preserve the logic of equal exchange in their own way.

> SCHOLIUM. With sharing economies, the notion of fair exchange is reattached to the time element, much more directly than in the case of local currencies. There is no formal unit of measure, no formal medium of exchange, and no store of

value. And yet, there is inevitably an informal calculation of equivalence, bearing on how much time goes into the services exchanged, or into developing the competence behind the necessary skills. In the absence of a formal currency, time itself becomes the informal currency. This retains capitalism's fundamental labor equation, time = money (T94, Strat. d). It actually attempts to make it more honest and live up to its own word by sidelining the exploitative element of profit. It brings into visibility that economic exchange is predicated on the capture of life-time, thus validating one of capitalism's basic mechanisms, while attempting to counteract its oppressive effects.

T26

There are many virtues to cryptocurrencies, local currencies, and sharing economies (with which things like Uber and Airbnb in fact bear no relation). As part of an ecology of alter-economic endeavors, they all have a role to play in constructing a postcapitalist future. However, *none can be said to revalue value.* All repeat, each in its own way, essential characteristics of the capitalist equation.

T27

The speculative engine of *surplus-value might provide a model for the revaluation of value.*

SCHOLIUM. The key to revaluing value might reside in reverse engineering a dynamic that is carried to its highest power in the most advanced, and seemingly regressive, segment of the capitalist economy: the financial markets. It may be necessary to go right for the heart in order to drive a stake through it, so as to make vitality live up to its potential (or potential live up to its vitality).

T28

What is a quality of life, construed as a value? The answer is simple: a qualitative life value is something that is *lived for its own sake*; something that is *a value in and of itself, in the unexchangeable "currency" of experience.*

> SCHOLIUM. A *life-value* has value to the exact degree to which it is incommensurable with any other experience. It is the singular color of an experience, such as it is, all of its own, that makes of it a life-value. In fact, a quality of life has value in exactly the way we say a color or a sound has a value. It has the value of the *qualitative character* of its own occurrence.
>
> > Lemma. The use of the word "occurrence" is not gratuitous. Quality of life, as a value lived for its own sake, is *evental*. To reclaim it amounts to folding the nonchronological time of capital back into the eventfulness of life's qualitative in-the-making.

T29

A life-value is a surplus-value of life.

T30

Capitalist surplus-value, like all surplus-value, including surplus-value of life, is defined by the generation of an excess of effect. It's all about *leveraging* (to use an ugly economic term for something that, like the surplus-value it produces, has a much broader pro-cessual scope and is not confined to the economic realm).

> SCHOLIUM A. In leveraging, output does not observe a linear relation to input. Effect is incommensurate with cause. This can occur because the effect is emergent. It spins off from its

conditions without being completely determined by them. A leverage effect embodies a *more-than*. Its occurrence cannot be explained by any particular underlying factor, because what it spins off from is the way in which multiple factors come together: it is an irreducibly *relational* effect that comes to more than the sum of its contributory parts.

T31

The leveraging of surplus-value is an *intensification* of process.

SCHOLIUM A. The generation of capitalist surplus-value through the *wage relation* is the classic example of leveraging, taken in the broadest sense as the extraction of a relational more-than. The excess of value skimmed off from the work process is more than a simple equation between the cost of the labor time put in and the market price of the resulting product. It arises from an intensification of the labor process: from increasing "productivity" toward gaining a "competitive edge." It is the differential in productivity between a given enterprise and its competitors that yields capitalist relative surplus-value. The means employed to carve out this performative differential is what Marx referred to as the "extortion" inherent in the wage relation.

SCHOLIUM B. The intensification of the labor process is the result of multiple, interacting factors belonging to heterogeneous formations and levels of life, having to do with qualitative differentials, including a good many exterior to the factory floor or corporate office. These bear on everything from educational background, training, team-building strategies, personal and professional time-management skills, motivational factors of all kinds, the development and deployment of technologies of attention, the transportation system enabling efficient commuting, patterns of migration bringing workers to the labor market and, last but not least, what the workers do in their off time that leaves them more or less labor-ready and enhances or vitiates their performance during work hours. There is *a plethora of contributory factors, whose tentacular reach snakes into every corner of life.* Profit sums up in a single number the integral way these contributory life-wide factors come together to produce a quantitative more-than.

> **Lemma.** The intensity of a process pertains to the *spread of qualitative differentials* it integrates: how far and in what way it sends its feelers into the crannies of the field of life.

T32

Profit is a surplus-value of life before it is an economic value.

> **SCHOLIUM.** Profit is a quantification of the way in which a certain complex of life-factors have come together to spin off an excess productivity-effect, which in the end is black-inked into the ledger in the numerical form of a return on investment. Profit marks the *conversion* of life-quality into what really counts in the capitalist system: economic quantity under perpetual increase. Corporate ledger books, and on a wider scale economic indicators, are indexes of this conversion. They are indicative signs of the economizing *capture* of surplus-value of life. The capitalist capture of surplus-value of life is an appropriation. By the time it hits the ledger books, it has been converted into private property.

T33

The wage relation is just one example of the generation of capitalist surplus-value. In a rapidly automating economy, its de facto primacy is increasingly threatened. On the internet and in the financial markets, surplus-value is generated directly as a relational movement effect. This suggests the concept of *surplus-value of flow.*

SCHOLIUM A. On the internet, the relational movement effect is generated by the way in which heterogeneous tendencies complexly play off of each other, spinning off monetizable trends captured through *data mining.* The profit generated is a quantitative expression of the life-wide cross-contagion between flows of affect, attention, and appetite. The surplus-value of life it captures is a surplus-value of flow. The quantity of profit skimmed off bears little relation to the formal input of time, labor, and investment. Consumers become informal producers, limitlessly contributing their life-time and vital activity, not to mention their donations of fixed capital in the form of data-minable devices. The resulting meme-effects may leverage returns exponentially. This widening disproportion between input and output consequent to surplus-value of flow is a major reason the labor theory of value must be reconsidered.

SCHOLIUM B. The concept of surplus-value of flow is an extrapolation from Marx's analysis of interest-bearing capital as money "already pregnant with surplus-value," such that the profit generated "is not the result of the act of purchase, the actual function that it performs here as money, but rather of the way in which this act is connected with the *overall movement* of capital" (Marx 1991, 463; emphasis added). This idea of the "pregnancy" of an act with surplus-value is generalized here to cover all movements plying the capitalist field, as they phase between the immanent outside of potential and take-up by apparatuses of capture. The pregnancy with surplus-value is pregnancy with potential, primed for relational emergence-effect production. Under neoliberalism, surplus-value of flow takes on an increasingly central role, as turnover accelerates and more and more sectors are catapulted into movement by globalization. This growing importance expresses itself in an obsession among investors for *liquidity*. The generalized concept of surplus-value as pregnantly connected with the overall movement of process can be designated by the name *machinic surplus-value* (Deleuze and Guattari 1983, 232–35). Machinic surplus-value is a synonym for surplus-value of flow emphasizing its imbrication with computerization and automation.

SCHOLIUM C. The move beyond the labor theory of value is present in embryonic tendency in Marx's own work. The concept of machinic surplus-value as proposed here radicalizes Marx's analysis in his famous "Fragment on Machines" (Marx 1993, 670–711). Marx analyzes automation as the objectification of the "general intellect," whereby "social knowledge" becomes "a *direct force of production*" (706; emphasis added). More than that, "powers of social production have been produced, not only in the form of knowledge, but also as *immediate organs of . . . the real life process*" (706; emphasis added). The "immediate organs" are automated machines: "self-acting mules," he wryly calls them (706). Although Marx himself does not go so far, it is clear from the vantage point of the digital future he did not live to see that when the distributed ("overall") movements of the "real life process" become a "direct force" autonomously driving the production of surplus-value—thanks to the self-acting code mules let loose upon the world by Silicon Valley to work the global data mines—the correlation of surplus-value to "necessary labor-time" is attenuated to the breaking point. Marx himself intimates as much: "Capital itself is the *moving contradiction,* [in] that it presses to reduce labor time to the minimum, while it posits labor time, on the other side, as sole measure and source of wealth. Hence *it diminishes labor time in the necessary form so as to increase it in the superfluous form*"

(706; emphases added). Today, the increase in the "superfluous" form (unanchored from "real labor" and "real wealth") comes most dramatically in the nonhuman form of the automated data mining of our online movements on social media and the internet in general. Here, the diminishment of necessary labor-time tends to the infinitesimal limit. The human input is contracted into the thinness of a click. With each click, we are hard at "work," even in leisure, for the production of capitalist surplus-value, all the while absorbed in our real-life process and its intensifying relational reticulation through ever-densifying social media.

> **Lemma a.** In the digital world, surplus-value of flow is synonymous with *surplus-value of information*.

> **Lemma b.** The *financial markets* operate on surplus-value of flow, in exemplary fashion. They, too, leverage differentials.

SCHOLIUM D. Financial derivatives are pure operators of surplus-value of flow. "They are commodities that exist purely within circulation" (Bryan and Rafferty 2007, 148). "They are products of circulation, not significantly of labor" (Bryan and Rafferty 2006, 154).

T34

The leveraging of differentials is a characteristic of the capitalist process at all levels.

> **Lemma a.** The analysis of the differential mode of operation of the capitalist process has far-reaching consequences for a number of core issues, including capitalist subjectivity, class, the status of the "real" economy, and even the nature of the human in relation to capitalism.

SCHOLIUM A. For the financial markets, the differentials take the form of spreads between economic sectors, national currencies, financial instruments, and most especially time intervals, as a function of which all of the other differentials fluctuate. The differentials are in overall movement relative to one another over time (T18). The financial markets game the differentials—none more than the *time differential*—toward the generation of surplus-value of flow (Knorr Cetina and Preda 2007).

SCHOLIUM B. Capital comes in many forms. It is not confined to the financial markets. It comes in forms other than investment money and financial instruments. Labor, to the extent that it is used to leverage an excess-over, is a form of capital ("variable capital" in the Marxian vocabulary). Equipment used to gain a competitive edge is also capital ("constant capital"). As is copyright-protected intellectual property used to unlevel the informational playing field. Prestige value, such as star status, is leveraged as a form of social capital. Reputation is another leverageable form of social capital, both in its traditional and emerging online forms. By neoliberal reckoning, an individual human being itself is a form of capital. The financial markets play the differentials between all of these forms of capital, and more.

> **Lemma b.** Under neoliberalism, an individual human being figures as *human capital*.

SCHOLIUM C. An individual is human capital to the extent that it manages to locally embody the overall movement of capital. The individual dips into the flow in such a way as to fashion its person as a miniaturization of the overall movement. Its life-activity becomes a quantum of capitalist surplus-value to its self-driving core. Its job is to *surf the movements of capital*: to make itself competitive across the successive waves of the rapidly changing job market, or as an independent entrepreneur (the preferred choice for "millennials" who are in the loop). This life-surfing fashions the individual as an ambulant personification (T67 Schol. c; T68–T69) of surplus-value of flow. The individual's job description is its life description: to strategically play the qualitative differentials that compose its field of life. These include, among others, the differentials between leisure time and work time, skill development and the application of acquired knowledge, friendship and networking, discipline and improvisation, energizings and replenishment, immediate satisfaction and tactical deferral. A fundamental task is to glean surplus-value of information and leverage it. This involves producing surplus-value of perception (Massumi 2014a; T34 Schol. e), not to mention surplus-value of sociality—a whole spread of qualitatively different surplus-values. The dynamic bundling of these different surplus-values composes the integral surplus-value-of-life that characterizes the individual as human capital. It is ultimately this surplus-value of life that is captured by the capitalist process. A unit of human capital is a quantum of surplus-value of life subsumed under the overall movement of capital as a function of its own dynamic self-driving. One is captured by one's own perpetual movement of self-fashioning. Human capital was invented by neoliberal capitalism to replace the figure of the worker in *an attempt to render obsolete the antagonism between worker and capitalist* that structured the preceding industrial phase of capitalism. What better way than to make the capture by capital self-acting? To make the individual's becoming-itself a capital equation? The ongoing neoliberal project of disabling that antagonism flattens capitalist subjectivity into a single figure: the "entrepreneur of oneself" (Foucault 2008, 224–26). This project is successful to the degree to which *complicity* becomes the fundamental mode of existence of the life of the individual in the capitalist field, at every level of society. The ensnaring complicity of the *creditor–debtor relation* replaces the worker–capitalist antagonism as the dominant differential tension. This internalizes what was an antagonism marking the outside limit of the system (a potentially fatal "contradiction" in the traditional Marxian vocabulary) into an economic operator fully within its orbit, entirely subsumed to its logic. The creditor-debtor relation is the black sun around which the neoliberal production of capitalist subjectivity comes to revolve (Lazzarato 2012, 2015).

> **Lemma c.** The ability of financial capital to leverage the spreads between other forms of capital, extracting surplus-value of flow from their complex pattern of movements, gives it a power of overflight that makes it *meta-capital* (Bryan and Rafferty 2006, 13).

SCHOLIUM D. Financial capital is the epitome of capital, carrying what it can do, as driver of surplus-value, to the limit. In the neoliberal economy, the financial sector takes off from the "real" economy. It unleashes surplus-value of flow at the meta-level, declaring its independence from the "underlying assets" of the productive economy. Financial capital's autonomization of surplus-value of flow takes the form of derivatives such as options, hedging, and credit default swaps. With options and hedging, profit is made from speculating on ups *and* downs of the movements of underlying assets, *capitalizing on volatility itself*. With credit default swaps, secondary financial instruments are constructed by dividing and recombining existing assets ("tranching"). The idea is that a strategic mix is more secure than an unbundled collection of the same assets because the lowest-grade assets can default without bringing the whole house of cards falling down (this is "securitization"). However, with the trading of the bundled assets, a new tier of assets is created, in a wholly derivative way, without anything new being produced—aside from the ability of the new financial instrument to circulate independently. The value of the derivative can fluctuate in a way that is largely unanchored not only from the ownership of any underlying assets, but also from their individual valuations (Bryan and Rafferty 2006, 10–13, 18, 37, 52, 66, 74–75, 129, 154, 184). Securitization segues into pure speculation. In reality, the underlying "assets" are not necessarily assets in any normal sense of the term. In the case of credit default swaps, they are debts (mortgages, car loans, and student loans being the prime—or subprime—examples). The secondary debt market performs the capitalist magic trick of making debt a credit instrument, in ways far more powerful (leverageable) than simple interest-bearing capital. The very distinction between an asset and a liability is erased at this meta-level of capital, along with the significance of the distinction between productive and unproductive economic activity. At this level, capital is effectively *self-abstracting* from the "real" economy. Financial capital can never untether itself entirely from the productive economy. But the fact that under neoliberalism it is the leading economic sector (the value of the financial markets far exceeds that of the productive economy) is highly significant. The emphasis on financial capital is in fact one of the key defining characteristics of neoliberalism. The neoliberal economy is increasingly anchored in the tendential unanchoring of financial capital from the productive economy. The tables have turned, to the point that *it is the productive economy that might more accurately be considered secondary to financial capital.* The two realms of the capitalist economy still revolve around each other, but the power relation has shifted, turned upside down. This self-turning of capitalism on its own head vastly increases volatility . . . which only further feeds the ability to game surplus-value of flow, actually strengthening the financial sector, which up until now has been able to skate past the periodic crises that inevitably result. The workhorse of industrial capital has been displaced by the cat of financial capital. Neoliberalism repeatedly throws the economy into the air, trusting it to land back on its feet (onto the backs of the self-acting mules it rides). Under neoliberalism, in Herman Minsky's oft-quoted dictum, the high-risk surfing of volatility has become so integral to the economy that it is now the case that "stability is destabilizing" (Minsky 1982, 26). Seen in this light, the jargon of "securitization" seems like a bad capitalist joke.

> **Lemma d.** Nevertheless, an alter-economy that takes off from the model of finance rather than that of currency might be able to postcapitalize on the logic of derivatives—taken more broadly than in the narrow economic sense (Martin 2015) and in potentializing connection with the notion of surplus-value of life—to leap *beyond productivism* and the grindstone *paradigm of work* (T91 Schol. b; T94 Schol. d) that forms a bond of enemy-brotherhood between capitalist and traditional Marxist political economy. Such a project would move instead toward a *paradigm of creative play* (T94, Strat. c).

SCHOLIUM E. The *digital automation* of financial trading intensifies the role of surplus-value of flow by accelerating data analysis and, as a consequence, the speed of turnover of financial transactions. This boosts capitalism into hyperdrive. Surplus-value production effervesces. Machinic surplus-value production overall asserts greater and greater autonomy from its would-be human masters' conscious control. It is important not to forget that other forms of surplus-value are co-involved in this phenomenon. There are always decision points or pressure points where human intervention is desired or necessitated. Given the superhuman complexity of the movements under way, and the inhuman speed of their turnover, the intervention cannot employ the means that the human has traditionally used to define its exceptionalism: deliberative ratiocination, methodical rationalism. Both day traders and floor traders speak of heightened or altered states of attention and perception, often articulated in terms of "gut feeling" or intuition (Lee and Martin 2016, 79, 90, 134, 245, 271; Knorr Cetina and Preda 2007, 132). These are *surplus-values of perception.* They capitalize on a self-acting excess-over the normal state of perception and the manner in which, under normal circumstances, it feeds deliberative thought and decision-making. The gut generation of surplus-values of perception, directly articulated with the complex movements of finance with a view to the extraction surplus-values of flow from them, is a way in which the *human strives to become equal to the machine.* The "human" intervention must strive to enact a *becoming-machinic of the human* (paradoxically, through intuition). The human is annexed to the machinic process. This is an exemplary case of the "real subsumption" by capital of human life and capacities whose general form, at the core of neoliberalism, is human capital. The neoliberal concept of human capital is explicit about its becoming-machinic. Human capital, in the words of one of neoliberalism's founding fathers, is based on "an all-inclusive concept of technology" that encompasses the "innate abilities of man" (Schultz 1971, 10). The individual human being becomes a humanoid vector of machinic surplus-value production: a two-legged self-acting mule.

SCHOLIUM F. The neoliberal subsumption of human life under capital that peaks on the trading floor, and is embodied more broadly in human capital, is the culmination of a process that has run through human history. It makes palpable something that retrospectively appears to have been the case all along: humans are not the masters of the capitalist process. They are captives of it, down to their own self-fashioning. *Humans do* *not run capitalism; capitalism runs through the human.* Humans do not direct its development; its self-driving annexes their becoming. Human capital is the self-accomplishment of capitalism as a power formation.

> **Lemma e.** This is another way of stating the truism that *the differential between the human and the machine* is pivotal to capitalist dynamics, and that "human nature"—which is in fact human-becoming always-in-excess-over any stable nature it may claim for itself at any given time—is entirely bound up with the playing out of this differential.

T35

Capitalism is a *more-than human of the human.* It is a processual driver of human becoming.

T36

In spite of this—or rather because of it—there is no sense in lamenting the ascendancy of financial capital over the financial economy, as if one were more real and more human than the other, and therefore morally superior. *The path to a postcapitalist future is not to be found in rescuing the good old "real" economy* from the bad new economy of "fictitious" capital.

> SCHOLIUM. By what standard of measurement is the extortion of labor upon which the "real" economy is based "better" than the human-capital subsumption of life associated with the financialization of the economy? Both are regimes of power that capture and mutilate life.

> **Lemma.** Embrace the more-than human of the human (Manning 2016). Turn it. Deviate its becoming.

T37

The primacy of the time differential makes futures the paradigmatic financial instrument. Ultimately, *it is the future that is captured by capital.* The capture of the future is the capture of potential, change, becoming. Such is the power of finance.

SCHOLIUM. The forms of financial capital discussed earlier are species of futures, in the extended sense.

T38

The differentials that are leveraged through speculative finance index *qualitative life differentials.* The change in the economic numbers over time indexes the way in which qualitative life differentials play themselves out. Capital games that play.

SCHOLIUM. For example, fluctuations in national currencies, so fundamental to the hedging strategies regularly used by corporations to act upon the future, reflect differentials in quality of life and political power among developed economies and developing (or unraveling) economies. Differentials of this kind are collective, bearing on populations. They are relational, bearing on the way in which the individuals composing those populations actively come together to form a complex, ever-fluctuating field of life. They are restlessly *transindividual.* When a price is made on the trading floor, an interval of field-fluctuation peaks in a single quantified data point. The changing relationality of the collective spread funnels into the registering of a single discrete quantity, fixed in the books once and for all: captured. The *n-dimensioned heterogeneity of the life factors* conditioning this capture is reduced to the one dimension of the economically registering profit-point. The transindividuality of the field of life channels into a punctual event of accumulation, individually owned. An n-dimensional ecology that is everyone's and no one's (that is "common") is packaged into a possession, enclosing the wide-open world of life-relation in a private appropriation. This is the perpetually replayed "tragedy of the commons," which is not a historical phase of capitalism but its permanent modus operandi, summed up in the word "accumulation."

> **Lemma.** The production of *all surplus-value is transindividual,* in that it involves turnover, and the turnover is conditioned and energized by qualitative differentials spread throughout the field of life. The financial markets are just one example, albeit a privileged one.

T39

Capitalism is *coextensive with economization* (T18 Schol. a; T22 Lemma a): the process by which the qualitative field of life is economically appropriated and subsumed under the principle of perpetual quantitative growth.

T40

Understanding the economic *system* is one thing. Understanding the *process* of life's economization through which the capitalist system's operations feed themselves, as an apparatus of capture, is quite another.

T41

Speaking about "the economy" *as if it were a self-sufficient system* with set "needs" that must dictate to life, and must be given precedence in governmental reasoning, is to ignore its status as an apparatus of capture: a self-feeding system opening onto a wider processual field, whose differential flows and energies it uses to power itself.

> SCHOLIUM. The economy is an *open system* (T11). It needs its

immanent outside of the field of life more than its immanent outside needs it (which is not at all), because it is nothing other than the process of appropriating the potentials to be found there. Economization depends on the life-field's fluctuating n-dimensional spread for the creation of the qualitative differentials it quantitatively mines. In a postcapitalist future, the tables will be turned. Life will dictate its qualities to the economy.

T42

There is a crucial *difference in nature between intensity and quantity* that needs to be factored into the account of the economization of the field of life. Surplus-values are creatures of intensity.

SCHOLIUM A. A surplus-value, it was said earlier, is an emergent effect that is relational: it comes of the singular way a multiplicity of contributory elements come together to spin off a collective effect. The effect has a quality of its own that it owes, genetically, to the qualitative differentials between its conditioning elements. But it does not reproduce those differences. It spins off into its own singular character. It adds its own difference to them. The singularity of the emergent effect is not reducible to the contributory parts, even in aggregate. It is more than the sum of its formative parts. It is in self-additive excess over them. The emergent excess-effect's singular quality brings to expression the *intensity* of its contributory factors' coming-together: it culminates the playing out of the *tension* inherent in their qualitative differentials. It expresses, in and as its own emergence, the way that the tension holds more potential in itself than the linear causal connections among the contributory elements could ever claim credit for. This is a creative tension. The contributing elements can, of course, be numbered. But it is not their quantity per se that has intensity. It is their *manner* of coming integrally together that has an intensity. The intensity expresses itself in a *supplementation* of their number: the emergence of an excess-effect. The expression of intensity is supernumerary. It is important to hold on to the idea that *intensity does not express itself.* It is expressed in an emergent quality that supervenes upon (comes self-creatively in addition to) the contributing factors' number, and which counts as "one" on its own account, in the manner in which it singularly affirms its own character. "The many become one and are increased by one" (Whitehead 1978, 2).

> **Lemma a.** Intensity is *immanent to expression.* It is *enveloped* in the expressed quality that spins off from it. It is not itself expressed as such. Intensity belongs to the immanent outside of the field of emergence.

> **Lemma b.** Because intensity does not express itself, except in what emerges from it, it is *easily annulled.*

SCHOLIUM B. The primary mechanism for the annulment of intensity is undue explanatory trust conferred upon quantification: the mistaken belief that the count of a field of emergence's participating elements can be explanatorily substituted for their creative tension. Attempting to grasp intensity and the potential it harbors through quantitative analysis amounts to *misconstruing the immanent outside as external*: as an exterior standing in opposition to an interior. This in turn amounts to eliding the difference between processual ecology and systemic environment. In a systemic environment, elements and operations can be treated as units, singled out and recombined, enabling counting and quantitative analysis. The systemic mobilization of quantification gives it awesome power. It builds this power by capitalizing on intensity, even as it explanatorily annuls it.

> **Lemma c.** Systems also harvest surplus-values.

SCHOLIUM C. Systems run on synergies: emergent, relational effects that raise a system's operation to a higher power. This is called *efficiency*. Efficiency is the intensification of a system through the production of a surplus-value of interaction between its parts that is carefully contained within the system's internal circuit of operations (this is why we tend to speak in terms of efficiency "boosts"). This internalizing capture of intensity is what gives systems their vitality. It is their life-line. It is their metabolism. It runs them. In capturing intensity, systems are availing themselves of processual potentials. They are systematically *dipping into process,* to boost their internal functioning. The annulment of intensity is never total. The annulment of intensity is the mark of its selective appropriation.

T43

Affect has to be factored in to arrive at a comprehensive account of the distinction between intensity and quantity.

SCHOLIUM A. Temperature provides a template for understanding the distinction between intensity and quantity, with attention to the place of affect. Compare eighteen degrees centigrade on a sunny autumn afternoon to eighteen degrees on a rainy day in spring. The temperatures are the same, but the weather conditions factoring into each are entirely different. Upstream of the registration of each temperature lies an infinity of factors belonging to qualitatively different registers and scales—friction between particles, rays and refractions and reflections of light, streams of wind, water evaporation, heat concentration and dissipation, and many others. It is the coming together of these factors that composes the state of the weather. More precisely, it is their differentials that compose it. The state of the weather spreads across them, taking up their many-dimensioned difference into itself, without erasing it. Rather, each weather state adds its own difference to theirs. It adds its unique emergent quality, arising as the resultant of their conditioning difference. Multiple contributory factors fold into the weather to make its global difference, as an integral emergence-effect. The way in which the factors come together to yield a spring temperature of eighteen degrees is entirely different from the way in which they come together to yield the same autumn temperature. We feel the difference. The two seasonal weather states affect us differently. They each integrate their conditioning factors in their own singular way. We feel their respective singularities. We feel cold in the autumn temperature and bask in the same spring temperature as the long winter begins to break. We are a part of the relational mix. Our affective state resonates with the conditioning factors, registering it on a purely qualitative scale. That scale envelops its own differentials. In its singularity can be discerned a number of mutually enveloped qualitative dimensions, also differing in nature one to another: seasonableness, comfort, the sense of the passage of time, bodily spring reawakening, a fore-hint of hunkering down for the coming winter. The differential of the multiple conditioning factors, as registered in a singular qualitative feeling integrating its own multiplicity of contributory differentials, is an *intensity*. Our affective state *resonates* with the intensity of the weather. Then the thermometer comes along and registers the same weather states on a numerical scale. It factors out the qualitative differences, funneling them into a single figure. The single figure does not explicitly register the singularity of the qualitatively different weather states. It annuls their singularities, blurring their compositional differences in the unicity of its own quantitative expression. It gives a *single,* definite expression to the *singular,* indefinite multiplicity of conditioning differentials of the great outside of the weather. It transposes their difference from their outside field of emergence onto a number scale showing them to be the same. On the temperature scale, the events' intensities are represented by an identical number. They can now be treated as equal, their differences bracketed. They have been calibrated. They have been rendered commensurable. They have been made comparable. They have come in from the outside, and now enter together, on an equal basis, into other compositional fields plied by systems operating in ways foreign to the weather in its home field. They can now figure for the science of meteorology—and the business of weather reporting and forecasting that spins off from it. The differences conditioning the two states are not erased from the history of the world. They are only annulled for the purposes of a new order of operations enabled by their now quantitative status. The contributory differences of the weather field do not go where numbers can. They cease to make the same kind of difference. Their translation into circuits in which numbers systematically travel makes them make a different difference. They have been converted. Their allegiances have changed. Our skin registers the singularity of the events as they happen. The thermometer gives them a sameness that makes them commensurable for all time. Affect resonates with qualitative intensity, in the field in which it occurs, sharing in its event. Measure converts qualitative intensity into a quantity, transporting it into a different field where it contributes to events of a nonweather kind (events of surplus-value of scientific knowledge production and the corporate capitalist surplus-value production tying into it). *Both the affective resonation and the measurement can be seen as emergent effects of the weather.* They remain in a certain relation. The measurement *indexes* the weather conditions. This enables the conversion to move in the reverse direction, for example from a weather forecast to our preparations for an outing. But in the reconversion, the eighteen degrees centigrade figures in a *general* way. The singularity of any given instance of eighteen degrees, and all of them en masse, have been translated into a general *indicator*. Even if the temperature forecast proves numerically accurate, it still will not express the affective reality of how our skin resonates with the conditions out in the field. Under certain conditions, we may still feel cold in eighteen degrees in the spring, experiencing an untimely hint of autumn. There is always an excess of emergence-ready qualitative conditioning over the captive accuracy of their quantitative indexing. *Affective resonance ultimately resists measure.* Relation is always more lively than its systematic registering. There is an excess of liveliness over any indexing of it. This lively remainder left over after capture is surplus-value of life.

Lemma a. Affect expresses intensity without annulling it.

Scholium b. Affect is an *immanent differentiation* of a field of intensity. It expresses the difference made by the differences composing the field. It does not separate itself from the field, even as it differentiates itself from its conditioning factors. Weather-affect stands out from the weather not in opposition to, but as a function of, our body's immersion in it. Affect is an immersive emergence-effect. It brings the qualitative differences of the field into emphasis in the field, expressing the singularity of its own immersive character.

Scholium c. The issue of affect's relation to intensity is intimately tied to the basic Spinozist definition of affect as the *"ability to affect and be affected."* This base definition must always be completed by the corollary that the playing out of an ability to affect and be affected coincides with the crossing of a threshold accompanied by a *registering of the feeling of that transition.* Affect comprises the differential between these two aspects. It involves many *subdifferentials* on each side. On the registering-of-the-feeling-of-the-transition side, the subdifferentials concern the way that an affective quality always includes a sense of another, related quality differing from it. The way a spring-like change in the weather can include an autumnal accent was one example. Another is the way that love and friendship always mutually include each other, in a patterned contrast having different emphases and activating different attractors, such that the differential between them plays out into different tendential orientations according to the case. On the ability-to-affect-and-be-affected side, the subdifferentials include things like contrasts of position, disposition, movement pattern, resilience, and plasticity. On that side, affect pertains to an intensive field. Back on the registering-of-the-feeling-of-the-transition side, it pertains to the coming to *expression* of the field's intensity. This two-sidedness gives the concept of affect a conceptual spread. The word affect can be used to encompass both sides, or it can be used to refer preferentially to one side or the other. "Intensity" can have the same spread, since affect does not separate itself from it but rather brings it to an emphasis of immanent expression. Accordingly, "intensity" can drift toward synonymy with "affect." Each time "affect" is used, it is important to be aware of the conceptual spread of its double-sided nature. Each time "intensity" is used, its imbrication with "affect" should be noted. In what follows, intensity and affect will mainly, but not always, be plotted to the two contrasting sides, with "intensity" referring to the field differentials of the affect-and-be-affected-side, and "affect" referring to the expressive registering-of-the-feeling-of-transition-side. The reason for this choice is that it allows for a juggling of agendas. When qualitativeness is being specifically addressed, the word "affect" will tend to be used, exploiting the fact that its resonating-with intensity remains purely qualitative. When the capacity of the field of emergence to lend itself to quantitative capture is being focused on, "intensity" will be used preferentially, because intensity can also *resonate with quantification* (T44 lemma; T46; T50 Schol. b), so that it makes sense to speak of "intensive magnitude" (T77). At times, the phrase "affective intensity" will be used to encompass both sides of the affect/intensity equation. These are not hard-and-fast rules. A certain forbearance, and terminological agility, will be asked of the reader.

> **Lemma b.** The temperature example, and the preferential use of the term "affect" to refer to the expressive registering-of-the-feeling-of-the-transition side of the equation, should not be taken to imply that affect is essentially a question of *human perception.*

SCHOLIUM D. The differentials whose tension spins off an integral affect as an emergence-effect registering the intensity of the field, immanent to its event, affect each other. Otherwise, they would not be in tension, and nothing would play out. In the weather example, the friction between particles, rays and refractions and reflections of light, streams of wind, water evaporation, heat concentration and dissipation that spin off into an affective registering of their field of co-occurrence, *register each other.* It is their registerings of each other that is integrated into the global feeling registering the overall movement of the weather event they co-compose. The friction between particles registers heat, evaporation registers heat concentration, heat concentrations register rays of light, wind currents dissipate heat. Affect figures on this level *independent of the human.* This is *nonhuman experience.* This nonhuman experience re-figures in our experience, through the added difference of our affect's singularity. That singularity integrally envelops the multiplicity of the nonhuman affects. It is both monadic (as is each enveloped subaffect) and constitutively open: it can only bring the field to this singular expression because it is formatively immersed in it, arising from a participation in it.

T44

Affect resonates. Measure indexes. These two modes are processually interlinked, across their difference.

> **Lemma.** This difference in mode of operation marks a difference between two orders, one directly qualitative, the other built upon quantification. Between the orders there is both separation and connection. Separation, because their modes of operation are incommensurable. Connection, because they are linked by a process of conversion, so that one indexes the other. The two orders stand in *disjunctive articulation* with each other, neither identical nor opposite: different in nature but processually linked. Both register, in their own ways. In addition, quantification registers the qualitative, in its own general way. (For more on the complexities of the relation between quantity and quality, see T79.)

T45

Quantification involves *generalization*.

> **SCHOLIUM.** The qualitative order concerns singular sets of circumstances, whereas orders built upon quantification concern general ideas. *General ideas* are those that subsume more than one singularity under a single umbrella and apply themselves equally to each, in such a way as to sweep them up together into different systems circuits. This was seen in the way the same temperature reading applied equally to the two qualitatively different states of the weather. General ideas are by no means all quantitative, but systematic quantification always generalizes.

> **Lemma.** The conversion of the qualitative into the quantitative is the *translation of the singular into the general.* The financial markets represent a highly significant exception to this rule (T46 Schol. b).

T46

The registering of the qualitative by the quantitative is by nature *reductive.*

> Scholium a. The full complexity of the conditions of the event from which the quantity is extracted is funneled down to a single, simple figure. There is an *essential excess* of difference, complexity, process, flow, and co-motion on the side of the qualitative that is never entirely absorbed into quantitative ordering. There is much that escapes conversion. There is a leftover of changeable qualities, of liveliness, that does not count, and remains unaccounted for. This can be analyzed under the concept of *bare activity.* When the terms "qualitative field of life" or "field of emergence" are used, they are referring to the immanence of the co-motion of bare *activity* to the *actions* (discrete operations) fed by its systematic capture. New kinds of complexity can be built on quantification and systematization, but these are of another order, leading away from the immediacy of the event, and the bare activity formatively stirring it, into other domains.

> Scholium b. Derivatives are exceptional in this respect. It is highly significant that in the case of derivatives, measurement is not effectively carried out as a separate operation that informs strategy from an outside perspective. The famous Black-Scholes equation used for pricing derivatives is widely recognized as flawed, both for its methodological circularity (Bryan and Rafferty 2013, 137) and for its outmoded reliance on probability as a way of notionally rationalizing the ineradicable contingency of volatility movements (Ayache 2010, 2016), and it is for this reason that in practice it is necessarily supplemented, if not supplanted, by feats of intuition (T34 Schol. e). What is significant is that the very structure of derivatives as financial instruments

is *in itself* a "computation" of differentials (Bryan and Rafferty 2007, 2013). The derivative instrument is designed to straddle in principle, a limitless range of differentials in such a way as to produce commensuration-effects. They do this by "binding" the present to the future in a pricing relationship, and by "blending" different asset forms in the same instrument, making them readily convertible (Bryan and Rafferty 2007, 140). This "intensifies" capital by intensifying the price relations between times and among different forms of capital. It also builds the computational aspect (the commensurating effect) into the very structure of the financial instrument, so that it becomes operative in the act of speculation. This blurs the distinction between capital as surplus-value and money as general equivalent or operator of quantification (this is what is meant by "meta-capital"; T34 Lem. c). This is on top of the intensification that comes with derivatives' blurring of the distinction between assets and debts (Bryan and Rafferty 2007, 141–42; T34 Schol. d). With derivatives, "capital itself creates and evaluates its own performance" (Bryan and Rafferty 2013, 135), intensely self-computing, in the act. "The only computational theory of the [financial] market is the market itself" (Ayache 2016, 240). Quantification collapses into the performance of the speculative act. It becomes self-applying, in the speculative event. This means that affective resonance—the registering of the volatile intensity of the economic "weather conditions"—converges with the machinery of quantification (as if the thermometer blew wind). In other words, derivatives are a special case where *quantification itself tends toward becoming-immanent to the capitalist field,* in an asymptotic movement that can never complete itself. With derivatives, the capitalist system tends toward the limit where the gap between system and process tendentially closes. This occurs as a consequence of the maximization of surplus-value of flow. Capitalist capture and mutant flow converge. Quantification rejoins the singular, becoming fully evental rather than reductively indicative. This is not an overcoming of capitalist capture, but a singular intensification of it.

> **Lemma a.** The computational status of the derivative in and as the event of speculation indicates that the opposition drawn above between quantification as generalization/reduction and the qualitative as singular/evental was too gross. It opens the possibility that practicable modes of quantification might be invented that cleave more closely to the qualitative field. These would index intensive magnitudes (T77), the complexity of the field's constitutive differentials as such, and the entering into continuity of the multiplicity of co-occurring contributory factors toward the production of a relational effect. Processually, to achieve this feat, the quantitative indicator would have to cleave so closely to the relational field that its indexing of the process would itself become a relational co-factor in the process, contributory to qualitative emergence. Philosophically, this becoming-immanent of the quantitative to the qualitative field might be thought of as a postcapitalist incarnation of the "numbering number" Deleuze and Guattari attribute to nomadic society (1987, 118, 389–94, 484–85). There are doubtless many aids for this becoming-processual of the quantitative to be found in qualitative mathematics and qualitative data modeling. Its possibility points in a privileged direction needing to be explored in alter-economic thinking and design (T94, Strat. 1).

SCHOLIUM C. Derivatives tend toward becoming-immanent, but can never complete that movement. This is attested to by the fact that the more intensely they operate, the more they separate off into a hermetic zone of "high finance" all their own, to such an extent that their very existence, let alone their nature, is barely suspected by the vast majority of people and is even little understood by the governmental institutions tasked with regulating the economy. It is as if they move in two directions at once: toward a field-convergence and just as vigorously toward separation as a particular sector of the economy, in a kind of synchronic oscillation. This tension is also found in the numbering number of nomadic societies, in a manner specific to those formations, in the spinning off from the field of relation of a "special body" of concentrated power (Deleuze and Guattari 1987, 392). In the case of derivatives, this is due to their being in the service of capitalist accumulation, which requires a periodic harvesting of profit by standard measure to confirm its success and "realize" itself. These operations are assured by the corps of financiers steering the financial sector. Deals close, prices are made, quantities of capital are fed back into other sectors, including the productive economy, in a step back from the limit. The irrational exuberance of pure speculative flow segues back into the prudential functions of hedging, arbitrage, and securitization (bracketing their predication on excess and the associated tendency of financial instruments to run away with themselves). Paradoxically, derivatives end up *separating their convergence* by fulfilling functions in the wider economy, as a particular sector of it. The convergence they effect between qualitative differential and quantification is re-separated from the qualitative field of life in its full expanse. In their own inimitable way, the operation of derivatives remains a separation-connection. The drive to accumulation they serve is like oil to the water in the sea of surplus-value of life (as it always is). Although neither general nor reductive in themselves, they interlink with economic functions that are both of these things, for which they provide a kind of adjacent hyperdrive, accelerating accumulation and flirting with crisis.

Lemma b. An alter-economy modeling itself more on

derivatives than currency can potentially emulate this convergence, contriving to close the gap as much as possible between intensity and measure, between the bare-active movements of the qualitative field of life and its quantification, their forces joined for singularity—but in a way that is not in the service of capitalist accumulation, eludes capitalist capture, and resists separating off the convergences fostered into a hermetic domain of power.

T47

Returning to the many more-classical (and neo-classical) realms of life and sectors of economy activity where the disjunctive articulation of the qualitative and quantitative is still in force in more orthodox forms of separation-connection, with the attendant operations of generalization and reduction—in these contexts the emergent complexity of quantitative orders are not only indicative, but applicative: they *apply themselves* to the qualitative field of life, as from without, in an attempt to make that field conform to a general modeling. They capture through application to the field.

SCHOLIUM A. To make the field conform means to channel its movements toward the reproduction of certain target forms and patterns. This reproductive *folding back* upon the field of emergence by orders emergent from it is a *regulatory* operation.

Lemma. The parameters of regulatory reproduction delineate *norms*.

SCHOLIUM B. The question of norms is enormously complicated. There is not one mode of power, but many. All are forms of capture, and the meaning of "norm"—or whether a given mode of capture is normative at all—has to be interrogated in each case. The specific cast of the capture has to be analyzed, as does the relation of that mode to others.

T48

There is an *ecology of powers* that needs to be attended to, with due attention to the interplay of value and norm.

T49

This question of the ecology of powers *cannot be separated from the critique of capitalism* and the imagineering of postcapitalist futures.

> SCHOLIUM A. This is because, once again, capitalism itself *is* a mode of power. It is a worldwide apparatus of capture, in all of its forms. Arguably, it is the only *universal* power formation (universal in the sense that it potentially extends to every geographical corner of the earth and into every cranny of life). As a power formation, capitalism bears an enormously complicated relationship to regulation and norms (T47, T51–52, T54–56, T63, T67, T71). Its status as a more-than-human driver of human becoming is in every respect bound up with the question of what evolving mode of power capital constitutes, and how it relates to other modes of power with which it shares the field of life, plying the same field of immanence—for there is only one. Capitalism integrates other power formations into its own operation, subsuming them without entirely erasing their difference in mode of operation (always leaving a qualitative remainder). Capitalism is ecumenical: it has no qualms about pushing itself to the limit in its speculative-finance dimension while continuing to host a range of other modes in its motley, global mosaic. Sorting it all out involves paying special attention to the way in which capitalism captures in different instances, what manner of separation-connections it contrives, and how their operation involves and/or exceeds regulation and norms.

SCHOLIUM B. None of this changes the fact that derivatives are the dominant mode of capital in the neoliberal epoch, both in terms of their dynamism and in terms of the magnitude of value they ferry. They have taken on the piloting role, forming the cutting edge of capital's running after surplus-value. This makes the logic of derivatives, as arcane as it may be, a necessary element in any consideration of capitalism as a power formation. Grappling with the complexity of derivatives is a privileged angle of attack for pushing further with the account of how quantity, intensity, and affect interrelate, the different ways in which qualitative differentials are integrated without being erased, and how and what manner of surplus-value (self-driving emergence-effect) is produced through that supplementation. This last point is crucial: it opens the question of how the logic of the derivative might be prior to and/or extend beyond the economic domain it currently dominates (without homogenizing).

T50

The range of the logic of the derivative can be conceptually extended by defining as a derivative *any emergent effect registering a complex qualitative differential.*

> **Lemma a.** Affective resonation was defined earlier as the purely qualitative registering of the intensity of the field of emergence from a situation of immersion in it: the integral way in which the contributory differentials constituting that field come together and play out to singular effect. Affective resonation is an *event-derivative.*

> **Lemma b.** It is toward the status of an event-derivative that financial derivatives asymptotically tend without ever fully arriving.

Scholium a. The term "event-derivative" is a synonym for surplus-value of life. An event-derivative is an affective registering of a field of emergence. It expresses the field's complexity, immanent to that field. It integrally envelops the field's intensity in its own difference, resonating with what it envelops. In doing so, it gives the field an *immanent emphasis,* like a peak rising from rugged foothills rolling to the tides of the distant sea, or a wave cresting above the roiling of the sea. An event-derivative stands salient, without separation. For example, the affect, composed of seasonableness, comfort, the sense of the passage of time, the bodily spring reawakening, the hint of the hunkering down for winter, that registers the singularity of a weather event is a lived quality expressing that occurrence of the state of the weather in the currency (or better, fluency) of experience. This surplus-value of life does not have the same form or content as the factors composing the conditions of emergence from which it derives (friction between particles, etc.). It envelops its conditions of emergence, and remains wrapped up with them, directly sharing in their event. But at the same time, it adds an affective dimension that asserts its difference in nature from them. The affective registering has its own quality, like the peak of a wave in contrast to the horizontal expanse of the ocean. The qualitative difference of the surplus-value of life is the differential feeling tone *of* the state of the weather: in and of it, but not it. An event-derivative, as surplus-value of life, is an emergent qualitative difference that *both envelops and is enveloped by* its conditions of emergence. It is an immersive effect. It is a participatory peak, a coiling wave. It remains in the qualitative register, in its own emphatic way.

Lemma c. Rather than a separation-connection, an event-derivative is an *accentuation-differentiation.*

Scholium b. On its own plane of financial capital, a derivative is an accentuation-differentiation of the market: enveloped in and enveloping its intensity (at the same time as the financial market itself is in tendential separation from the rest of the economy). The difference between derivatives and the example of the weather is that derivatives don't just register the market's intensity, they intensively *make the market* (Ayache 2010). Their speculative acts are the events that constitute it: not just enveloped and enveloping but *effectively* both, in one. This effective reciprocity of intensive making and the registering of intensity collapsed in the same speculative act offers an interesting model for alter-economic projects: evental auto-computation in affective resonance.

T51

In general/reductive mode, as in a thermometer reading, quantifying capture and conversion index the conditions leading to the formation of an event-derivative as surplus-value of life, but do so in a way that peels off into other domains, where other orders hold, and other system circuits move. From the vantage point of this separation, it can fold back down. It can be applied and reconnect. This indicative-applicative operation of separation-connection is the mark of the *second-order event-derivative*.

> **Lemma.** Second-order event-derivatives can also be called "*degenerate*" event-derivatives (in Peirce's sense of that term).

Scholium. The surplus-value generated by a second-order event-derivative is of another order than that of surplus-value of life. The quantitative event-derivative effects a conversion from qualitative surplus-value of life to *surplus-value of information*. It is the anticipated ever-more of information that drives the production of knowledge. Surplus-value of information is the technical analogue of the surplus-value of life, which it parallels in another register, exploiting the same conditions of emergence. When the results of the quantification are reapplied in regulatory fashion to the field of emergence, another event transpires. The second-order derivative folds back onto the field of emergence to reprime it. This regenerates a primary event-derivative or surplus-value of life, and the cycle repeats. Since the application is generally reductive, and the channeling regulatory, the intensity of the reprimed surplus-value of life is lesser (it effectively envelops fewer contributory factors, straddles fewer differentials, covering less of a spread). The lesser intensity of the reduced surplus-values of life produced when second-order event-derivatives re-event themselves in the field from which they derived is what earns them the label "degenerate." Peirce uses this word to denote a less intense mode of a category fundamental to process (for example, when a relation, or "thirdness," can be decomposed into a triangle of dual relations, or a "secondness" can be understood as a collection of individuals, these are degenerate forms of their respective categories in relation to a nondecomposable integral of three, or so close an embrace between two that they cannot be separated without their natures being destroyed). Even financial derivatives feed the formation of second-order event-derivatives, when they derive profit and feed it into other forms of capital and sectors of the economy, thus registering the effect of their exemplary mutant flows in the mainstream economic numbers.

T52

Capitalist surplus-value continually spins off *degenerate event-derivatives,* and in a way that constitutes an exercise of power.

SCHOLIUM. When the metrics associated with profit and capitalist surplus-value are reapplied to the field of life, the regulatory effect is the formatting of life as "human capital," or of the individual as entrepreneur of himself. Life activity is maximally channeled in keeping with the demands of capitalism's self-driving. Life activity becomes maximally subsumed under the capitalist process. The reductive effect is to convert the individual into an embodied *quantum of capital*, living to appropriate its own punctual profits (predominantly in the form of a yearly salary or an hourly wage). To the economic data-point there now corresponds a quantum of human life. The individual generates private profit, as part of a conversion cycle between its activity in the field of life and the system-wide quantification process. This conversion cycle drives the individual life as human capital. Ideally, the profit made is not all spent, but more importantly invested (in such forms as real estate and pension contributions). This feeds it forward into capitalism's self-driving. The feedback between the drive of human capital and capitalism's self-driving annexes the life of the individual to the capitalist process, as a quantized subset of it. It pools the individual life as an eddy in the great capitalist stream. The individual life is now a *degree of capitalist power* participating in capitalism's systemic power to animate itself (its self-driving dynamism; its machinic vitalism).

T53

The capitalist process is a more-than-human *subjectivity*.

SCHOLIUM A. Something that has developed the systematic power to animate itself, that has a self-driving dynamism, that exhibits a vitality of becoming, qualifies as a subjectivity. A subjectivity is defined by its power to self-produce and vary. Subjectivities are always open systems. Their self-driving is *self-relating*: they phase through thresholds of transition across which they qualitatively vary. Each phase gathers up the last into its own ongoing, which is always already prefiguring, or better, "preaccelerating" the next (Manning 2009, 5–7, 13–29). The phases are in a relation of differential mutual inclusion in nonlinear time, constituting a distributed, fundamentally noncognitive *memory*. The memory has two aspects: memory of the past (already realized potential stored in trace form) and *memory of the future* (the leftover of potential effectively fed forward for subsequent phases, preaccelerating them). The past memorial aspect is seen in capitalism in its motley preservation of formations from the past. This is important for understanding the heterogeneity of the power formations composing its ecology of powers, in which past formations are retained as "*archaisms with a contemporary function*" pressed, in one way or another, more or less directly, into the service of surplus-value production (Deleuze and Guattari 1983, 240, 251, 257–58).

Lemma a. Subjectivities are composed by *tendencies.*

Scholium b. Tendencies are *proto-subjectivities*: they are self-driving and self-orienting. The tensions between the qualitative differentials composing the field of emergence govern tendencies.

Lemma b. Capitalism is a *subjectivity without a subject.*

Scholium c. In capitalism, there is no peak-level integration. Rather than peaking out or plateauing, capitalism's self-integration no sooner weaves itself than folds back down into its field of emergence. It is in perpetual, self-relating processual turnover on its own conditions of emergence. In this perpetual subjective becoming, *there is no subject "become."* To think otherwise would be to hypostasize process (as is done, for example, when "society" is treated as if it were a holistic actant, an existing entity over and above the individuals and other factors composing it; or when a complex, distributed, relational process is treated as a "hyperobject"). This principle must be applied to the concept of class as well. The "capitalist class" is not an entity. It is not a holistic actant. It is a distributed systems operator whose special calling is to field the turnover of the capitalist process around its own cyclic self-constitution.

> **Lemma c.** What we call a *subject* is an integration of tendencies that is capable of being *taken for* and *treated as* a holistic actant. This is a matter of perspective.

> **Lemma d.** Applied to the human subject, the more adequate perspective is to treat the individual as a *dividual*: a composition of proto-subjective tendencies in tension and concertation (Massumi 2014b).

SCHOLIUM D. The individual human-capital subject is an integration of a differential array of subtendencies. At the same time, the multiplicity of human-capital subjects cohabiting the field of life are themselves subtendencies composing the higher-order integration of the capitalist system. The capitalist process moves through the levels. It is *transsubjective* and *transindividual*. If we restrict our attention to the self-consistency of the movements of becoming of a quantum of human capital (its phased self-driving, on its own level, as its own phenomenon), we are considering it as a *subject*. If we consider it from the point of view of the transsubjective movement of the capitalist process through it, we are seeing it as a *fractal region* of capitalism's subjectivity-without-a-subject (that is, as a dividual). The expression of a subject's fractality (dividuality) can be muted on its own level, creating the effective fiction that it is a discrete, separate entity. The job of *discipline* and *morality* is to model such effective fictions. They obscure the fact that, from the processual subjectivity-without-a-subject point of view, *all subjects are transsubjective and transindividual.* That is a necessary aspect of their composition, and a necessary dimension of their being in becoming.

Lemma e. There is *no such thing as a peak-level subject.* Accordingly, there is no such thing as a sovereign subject.

Lemma f. The role of affect as an "externality" immanent to and a formative factor in the capitalist field (T11) must be radically rethought in dividual terms, as a function of transindividual subjectivity-without-a-subject.

SCHOLIUM E. The subject's sandwiching between processual levels means that it is always in some way *subsumed* by the powers of integration moving through it. This means that *the subject is an effect of power.* It is the dependent effect of a higher integration. This is etymologically included in the word itself: *sub-jacere,* "under-throw."

SCHOLIUM F. These considerations of subjectivity are crucial for the imagineering of the postcapitalist future, and for the design of alter-economy projects meant to preaccelerate it. They change everything when it comes to issues of *decision* and "governance" (a fetish word for alter-economy projects involving cryptocurrencies based on developments coming out of blockchain technology). The intersection between the subject and transindividual subjectivity-without-a-subject is the intersection between *creativity and decision.* Everything depends on how that intersection is finessed.

T54

In the ecology of powers, regulatory operations that implant norms into the field of emergence constitute exercises of *biopower.*

SCHOLIUM. Biopower exerts a force of *normalization.* It attempts to direct what is arising from the field of emergence down regulated channels. To succeed in revaluing value, fully reaffirming the differential intensity of the field of life, the post-capitalist future will have to decouple value from normativity. It will have to grapple with disciplinary power and biopower. However, this is a necessary but not sufficient condition, because:

T55

There are also postnormative, nonregulatory foldings-back onto the immanent outside that are less modeling or channeling than inciting. With them, power moves beyond biopower to *ontopower* (Massumi 2015a).

SCHOLIUM. Ontopower operates by preemption. Preemptive operations dip into the field of emergence, taking the co-motional potential stirring there as their object. This is potential that has not yet taken determinate form. It is flush with the field of emergence. There is a margin of indeterminacy as to which existing modes of existence it might feed, or what forms of life it may emerge into. It is proto-formal: still a formative force whose conclusion is not foregone. It remains highly charged with the force of futurity. Because of this ontological indecision, the form-takings that will eventuate are struck with a high level of contingency. This makes the pokings of potential by preemptive mechanisms far less directive than normative channelings. Preemption *flushes out* takings-form of life potential. It is *incitatory*, piggybacking on the movements of emergence astir in the field. On the systemic level of neoliberal capitalism, these formative movements are captured in the fluid, eddying, ontogenetic (becomingful) form of human capital. There is much to be said about preemption that exceeds the limits of these theses. Suffice it to say that preemption cannot be glossed over, and also must be grappled with, through the invention of *counter-ontopowers.*

T56

With ontopower, power *exceeds regulatory functioning.* It is not for nothing that neoliberalism is obsessed with deregulation. Its power relation of human capital tends, at its intensest, toward the ontopowerful. Neoliberalism is integrally bound up with bio-power (or rather, biopower is integrally bound up with it) but at its ontopowerful cutting edge, it is aspirationally *postnormative.*

> SCHOLIUM A. An eddy of capital is just as self-driving, in its own small swirl of activity, as the capitalist economy as a whole. A quantum of human capital is actually less a separate subset than a fractal region. Since it is as manically self-driving as the overall movement that is the capitalist system as a whole, it runs on excess energies, and its excess energies can run away with *it.* The paradox of capitalism (speaking here specifically of neoliberal capitalism) is that its regulatory interventions in the field of life are wont to overspill, spinning off, as if by design, deregulated movements, even aberrant movements—*escapes.* Its exercises of biopower are applied as-if in order to overspill into ontopower. The regulatory force of the exercise of biopower gives the field of life a healthy modicum of sta-bility that prevents the escapes from tipping over into irrecu-perable crisis, or from heading off in postcapitalist directions. Ontopower takes processual precedence over biopower, with its intensified powers of production: its power to flush life out, inciting it into taking its own form, boosting it to self-produce as human capital (the word "produce" here takes on similar connotations as carried by the word "producer" in the enter-tainment industry). Human capital, at its intensest, is the most

direct mode of capture of the movements of excess fostered by ontopower. Biopower is commonly defined as a *power over* life (operating statistically on individuals as biosocial beings, and especially on populations of biosocial beings). Ontopower is less a power-over life than it is *a power-to generate a more of life*, a more-than of life. This is another way of saying that it is ontogenetic, a power not over beings but of becoming as such. Rather than channeling movements in the field of emergence, it *modulates* the bare activity (T46) constitutive of the field. Neoliberal capitalism, through its regulatory interventions, multiplies norms. At the same time, it unleashes an *overspilling of the norms* through its formatting of life as human capital.

SCHOLIUM B. This can be seen in the endemic, systemic corruption neoliberalism fosters (Hardt and Negri 2004, 178–79), as exemplified in such fractal personifications of capital as the Martin-Shkreli quantum (and before that, the Michael-Milken) and the Donald-Trump quantum (and before that, the Sylvio-Berlusconi). *But it can also be seen in a proliferation of the movements of escape of the kind discussed earlier, which take an unexpected turn and wind up affirming qualities of life as values in themselves, embracing primary surplus-value of life,* out from under its subsumption. These mutant turns reconstitute an immanent outside that undermines the system, as a function of the very process feeding it.

T57

The movements of escape composing neoliberal capitalism's immanent outside constitute a *primary resistance* to capitalism.

SCHOLIUM. The escapes that spin off from human capital involve the production of primary event-derivatives: an *autonomy* of creative advance, in immersive relation; an autonomous excess of relation releasing a quantum of ontopower unsubsumed by the capitalist process. Process *rewilding.*

T58

Notwithstanding the ubiquity and effervescence of movements of primary resistance that ontopower spins off, *ontopower lies at the heart of neoliberal capitalism.* It is what most characterizes it as a formation of power, as it lives itself out to its intensest, in pursuit of its aimed-at power-effect: the ever-intensifying economization of the field of life. Capitalism's heart, paradoxically, lies at its limit, where its system re-processes.

> Scholium. The *capture of ontopower* by preemptive mechanisms is the dominant mode of power under neoliberal capitalism, in the sense that it is the most intense, dynamic, and self-driving of its modes. Neoliberal capitalism builds itself on what systematically escapes it. For every quantum of autonomous creative advance, for every eventful quantum of primary surplus-value of life released, a corresponding quantum of capitalist surplus-value is prone to be captured for the system in the form of human capital. The two movements asymptotically converge in human capital, trending to its extreme. This word "extreme" is meant in the same sense as in the phrase "extreme sports": as thriving on intensities of risk and moving-with volatility and the contingencies it throws up. *Capture and rewilding go processually hand-in-hand.*

T59

The antagonism between the rewilding of potential and its preemptive capture as human capital is the *driving antagonism of capital under neoliberalism,* replacing the contradiction between the worker and the capitalist (and pivoting on the creditor-debtor relation as arena of struggle).

SCHOLIUM. This is not to say that the worker-capitalist antagonism has disappeared, or that class is no longer a factor in neoliberalism. The still-ongoing struggle in the 2010s in the United States for the fifteen-dollar-an-hour minimum wage, and the struggles over pension and health benefits playing out in such hot spots in the neoliberal wars as Wisconsin and Illinois in the United States, belie any such conclusion, as does the relentless push on the part of the Republican Party to increase the already gaping inequality in the system (Picketty 2014) by continuing to redistribute wealth upward to the richest tier, with the effective collusion of the Democratic Party (by its inability to offer an economic alternative). What it means is that the worker-capitalist dialectic can no longer be said to structure the capitalist field as a whole. This is precisely because it *is* an opposition, and oppositions are structural. Capitalism is not a structure. It is a system, constitutively open onto its immanent outside (ultimately, it is a process). An open, process-worthy system has no "whole" ("process-worthy" in the sense we say a ship is sea-worthy). It has global integrations of proliferating differentials. The integration emergently *adds itself* to the multiplicity of its conditioning factors, which it does not erase but rather supplements ("the many become one, and are increased by one"; T42 Schol. a).

T60

Given the processual embrace between the escapes of primary resistance and the captures of human capital, there is no getting outside of *complicity*.

SCHOLIUM A. Because capitalism is effectively universal

(potentially in force everywhere), piggybacked on every move affirming qualitative surplus-value of life in and for itself, there is the potential for a corresponding capture of capitalist surplus-value. This, however, does not mean that everything we do is "in" the capitalist system, in the sense of being completely determined by it. There is no "all in" the capitalist system, precisely because its process dips into an immanent outside (T11) in order to capture the potentials brewing there. Capitalism is aspirationally all-taking. But that does not mean that everything is completely given to it. The *origination* of potential belongs to its immanent outside. As an open system, it is to its outside that capitalism owes its own, derivative, creative powers. The mechanisms of capture of the capitalist process must reach into the immanent outside in order to extract a profit, and to generate a quantum of capitalist surplus-value to self-drive the system onward to an ever-next extraction. Once again, there is always a remainder of potential left over after this operation. The operation is a capture *of* autonomy. The neoliberal individual is a pivot point for *both* the generation of movements of escape and for their capture. *The individual under neoliberalism is powerfully complicit with capitalism by its very nature, and by the same token, it is in primary resistance to it, also by nature* (by virtue of its dividuality and the transindividuality that runs through it).

> **Lemma a.** Complicity is an ontological condition under neoliberalism. It cannot be avoided, but it is not all-defining. It should not just be critiqued. It should be *practiced* strategically, in ways aimed at always upping the ratio of escape over capture.

> **Lemma b.** In working toward a postcapitalist future, the key is *not critique.*

> **SCHOLIUM B.** Critique is important, but not as a policing of ideological or analytic correctness. In that role, it is a normative

mechanism that goes against the grain of the creative advance of capitalism, but in exactly the wrong way: in a way that does not effectively connect to its processual nature. Because of this, it misses the boat. It is already outrun by capital before it even finishes touting its own correctness. *Critique practiced as if it were a primary resistance is self-defeating.* This does not mean that it has no role, just that its role is not the sovereign role it too often arrogates for itself. Its role is the more modest one of assisting movements of escape by helping them scout out the terrain of the field of emergence, and shielding them by responding to arguments aimed at disarming them. Critique can provide backup for their primary task of self-affirming their qualitative difference, of carrying themselves to higher, tendentially postcapitalist, powers. It cannot, and should not, direct them.

> **Lemma c.** There is a need to embrace *creative duplicity*: emergent ways of strategically playing the ontological condition of complicity, to tendentially postcapitalist effect.

> **SCHOLIUM C.** Don't bemoan complicity—game it. Don't critically lord it over others with your doctrinal prowess—get creatively down and dirty in the field of play.

> **Lemma d.** Alter-economy projects need to consciously build in, and build on, creative duplicity.

T61

It is important to note that there are *directly qualitative* modes of normative power, and to build in resistance to these as well.

T62

It is even more important *not to overestimate* their power.

SCHOLIUM. Like the regulatory operations of biopower, qualitative modes of normative power figure importantly in the neoliberal ecology of powers. But the same thing has to be said of them as was said of worker/capitalist contradiction: they do not structure the capitalist field overall. Their dominance was a passing phase in the more-than human movement of capitalism, which has since undergone phase shifts carrying it into biopower, and beyond biopower into ontopower. This complicates what we mean when we speak of capitalist "oppression."

T63

The most well-known and best-studied qualitative mode of normative power is *disciplinary power*.

SCHOLIUM A. Classical disciplinary mechanisms attempt to *model* individuals in conformity with a pregiven set of target qualities—moral characters or ethical dispositions—that ought to guide their life activity. This is a process of *normation* (the best example of which is religious inculcation). Very different is *normalization* (Foucault 2007, 56). With biopower, normation shades over into normalization, losing its claim to dominance. Biopower is often equated with disciplinary power, but it is important to offset it from classical discipline, not least because it operates at its core by quantitative means. It is best considered a transitional form between classical disciplinary power and ontopower. But this transitional character does not mean that it doesn't have its own, self-affirming, qualitative difference. Under biopower, the norms are statistically derived, in a second-order quantitative treatment of the field of life that pools and systematizes the raw numbers. The results are *reapplied* to the field of life, through government and through the media, *in the name of quality of life*. Biopower is transitional in this sense as well, in that it explicitly combines a fundamental anchoring in quantitative analysis with a qualitative agenda. It attempts a double conversion, of the qualitative differentials of the field of life into statistical quantifications, and from these quantifications back into making a qualitative difference in that field. For example, the regulatory norms of healthy living are derived from measurement-data mined from the field of life and statistically processed. The results are then applied back down onto the field in a way meant to *channel*—rather than directly model—the population's ways of moving through life, with the aim of improving their quality of life. This is a "channeling," because even though the norms have a certain imperative force, they are not imposed wholesale. There is always a certain optionality to them. With regard to the individual, they are applied as *guidelines* or *nudges* (a concept that won Richard H. Thaler the 2017 Nobel Prize in Economics; Thaler and Sunstein 2009). They are also applied *environmentally,* which is to say in ways that modify the surrounding conditions of life, so that the guidelines suggest themselves implicitly, and the nudges go without saying. Biopolitical norms touch on some of the most intimate and everyday life movements, tendencies, habits, and concerns of the population. To the extent that they insinuate themselves into the very warp and woof of the life environment, they tend toward a becoming-immanent to the field of life, thus shading into ontopower. The norms are not straightforwardly applied. Their application has a *curve* to it. The treatment of the data yields a curve capturing the distribution of variations occurring in the field. The region where most data-points fall is *deemed* the normal range. We're talking bell curve. *The normal range is not pre-given.* It is derived, and it can change. It changes as the norms are reapplied to the field in ways that effectively channel life activity in what are considered healthier directions (or fail in that mission). The bell curve for things like heart health, the incidence of cancer, and life expectancy changes, and the norms are adjusted accordingly. The bell curve also changes as escapes from the norm, such as the North American opioid epidemic of the 2010s, run away with a significant portion of the population and alter its morbidity and mortality. In disciplinary normation, on the other hand, the norm is meant *not* to change, because it is based on purportedly timeless moral qualities of uprightness, or in less rigid varieties, on ethical precepts of goodness. They do change, of course, as escapes inevitably pool together into streams of cultural change in spite of normation. But each successive classical disciplinary modeling acts as if this hadn't happened, in denial of the fundamental fact of history (change).

> **Lemma.** A rule-of-thumb guide: disciplinary power *models,* biopower *channels,* ontopower *modulates.*

SCHOLIUM B. This is only rule-of-thumb because in the capitalist field these modes of power form *combinations and hybrids* (T65, T66, T67 Schol. c). As part of the ecology of powers, they are under continual, intercorrelated mutation. Their ratios and degree of intensity are continually shifting. It is to be assumed, given any particular period or empirical formation, that it is a question of a distinctive mix with unique compositional characteristics. Within that composition, the modes of power commingle as so many constitutive tendencies, as much in tension as in concert (in differential confluence). A processual-ethical evaluation (T6 Schol.) of the heterogeneous tendencies, their tensions, and their manner of coming together in spite of their tensions is necessary to understand the force of the overall power dynamic.

T64

It is important to factor into the mix classical disciplinary modes of power because even though they are archaic in the sense that they had their heyday in an earlier historical age and no longer characterize the overall regime of power today under neoliberal capitalism, they are still very much with us. They are *archaisms with a contemporary function* (T53 Schol. a).

SCHOLIUM. The contemporary function of resurgent norma-tion is to try to moderate, if not stave off, the relativizing power of biopower's normative drift and its segue into the deregulat-ing drive of neoliberal capitalist ontopower. Even more so, its aim is to stanch the escape from capitalist ontopower back to-ward the primary resistance of self-rewilding surplus-value of life. The processual intensification—the increase in powers of self-driving, or autonomization—is a trauma and a horror to normativity. It is passionately an affront to normation-based modes of life. But it is not without its horror for biopolitical nor-mativity as well, in spite of its becoming-environmental flirt-ing with it. Normation-based archaisms with a contemporary function are *reaction-formations* to what neoliberal capitalism's dynamism of creative destruction has unleashed. Such devel-opments as the rise of the religious right in the United States, to name just one of the fundamentalist movements agitating all of the world's religions (including of course Islam, and now even Buddhism, as seen in Myanmar), are reaction-formations against neoliberalism which take a moralizing route: the affir-mation of other-worldly values underwriting a rigid image of the upright moral character. Anti-immigrant sentiment and the economic isolationism as seen in the Brexit vote and else-where are further examples of disciplinary reaction-formation to neoliberalism, in these cases taking the sanctity of the nation as the transcendent principle of their moralism.

T65

Liberalism, in the social or political sense rather than the narrow economic sense, is also, in its own way, an archaism with a contemporary function.

SCHOLIUM. Attempts to revive the figure of the individual as responsible member of civil society embodying norms of "prosocial" behavior (the "tolerant neighbor," the "decent citizen") are also reaction-formations to the quasi-chaos of the excessive self-driving of the capitalist process under neoliberalism. They are not as rigidly moral as their religious-right nemeses, but still qualify as disciplinary. They oppose a soft disciplinarity to the right's hard discipline. They take the normative ethics route of inculcating a "good" disposition. Liberalism works by gently *molding* the character more than outright modeling it, as moralistic normation does. It appeals and appeases, strokes and pats on the back, to mold the social putty of the individual into the kind of well-regulated behavior in the public sphere that shores up the correspondingly well-regulated behavior of the liberal democratic state. Liberalism tries to stabilize the biopolitical bell curve by suspending quasi-disciplinary good-conduct weights from the top of the curve to prevent it from wobbling so much, and hold it better in place. The desired effect is to stanch the flow of primary resistance, channeling away from the radical temptation of extraparliamentary contestation and from the exuberance of the form of rewilding that goes by the name of queer, back into the well-oiled electoral wheels of the normative nation-state. The liberal nation-state is supple enough that it can try to coax these escapes back into its fold, by adding a special normative dispensation (for example gay marriage and other newly won, recognized rights) rather than out and out eradicating them. These are *soft captures.* Soft capture is the originality of liberalism, in its composing with discipline and biopower (liberalism does everything in its power not to recognize ontopower, but nevertheless co-composes with it through the normalization of the state of exception, which opens the door to the proliferation of preemptive mechanisms; Massumi 2015a). Liberalism, of course, composes with neoliberal capitalism, even as it works to attenuate its quasi-chaos (joining forces with human-capital narratives of personalization; T67 Schol. c). Its soft captures are, in effect, market extension mechanisms. They add to the neoliberal economy through the codification of new and proliferating niche markets. The originality of liberalism's soft captures drives what creativity liberalism has left at this late date in its history. Around them, the escapes continue, and even proliferate. Liberalism leaks.

T66

The *alt-right* recognizes the archaism of both of these types of reaction-formation (liberalism and classical moralisms), and with a vengeance. It counters them with a *proto-fascism* that has unpredictable powers of contagion.

> SCHOLIUM. At its fringes, the alt-right is alienated from the "establishment" conservatism of the religious right (as ensconced in the "mainstream" wing of the Republican Party in the United States) as well as from liberalism, for whose softness it nurtures a special hatred, in no small part because of the way it makes room for new rights, and the proliferation of leaks it grudgingly tolerates. The alt-right is not conservative in any traditional sense. It is *neo-reactionary*: it embraces its role as a reaction-formation, and plays it to the hilt. It bears a special kinship with archaisms-with-a-contemporary-function operating with hard-disciplinary normation—especially as regards the patriarchal model of masculinity. But it can in no way be reduced to those classical normative moralisms. The alt-right

prides itself on its in-your-face "political incorrectness." It tends to superimpose that model of dominant masculinity onto the charismatic leader, and the figure of the charismatic leader onto the head of state, and assimilate both to the everyday figure of the bully (Reid 2017). Its superimposition onto the nation-state structure annexes notions of ethnicity to the model of masculinity. The result is a racism as intense, if not more intense, than the misogyny that goes along with masculinist supremacism. The proto-fascist quality of this formation inheres in its *powers of contagion:* its power of unregulated becoming. This proliferative power makes the alt-right a strange *alloy of the classical disciplinary regime and ontopower;* of extreme top-down oppression, unleashed from traditional standards of moral uprightness, and emergent primary resistance. It is beyond the scope of these theses to plunge further into this morass in a way that would do justice to its creativity and complexities (such as variants that do not recognize the sovereignty of the nation-state). No alter-economic project, however, can afford to ignore it. No account of the ecology of powers can dispense with an analysis of proto-fascism and fascism: this short gloss is meant only as a placeholder for that analysis.

T67

Another directly qualitative mode of power, related to the other modes, is the *capture of affect as emotion.*

SCHOLIUM A. This capture is constitutive of the *personal,* as the proprietary dimension of the individual subject considered (and considering itself) as a discrete, separate entity. *Personalization* is a synonym for the capture of affect for the constitution of the proprietary dimension of the subject. Personalization bears a privileged relation to economization. Arguably, it does not exist outside processes of economization. Certainly the subject as we know it (commonly referred to as the "bourgeois individual," mini-sovereign of its own private domain) is a creature of capitalist economization and does not exist outside of it. It is clear that the subject as separate, self-subsistent entity, rather than a self-avowedly integrally-relational being-becoming, does not exist in indigenous societies. Neither did it exist, for entirely different reasons (having to do with the ferocity of the integral subsumption of all movement under a regime attempting by any means necessary to peak out in a maximally sovereign oversubject) in non-European despotisms or the monarchisms of Europe as tendentially driven by their processual ideal (attractor state) of the absolute monarchy (Dean and Massumi 1993). It will necessarily be the case that the personal, pseudo-sovereign subject *will have to go extinct in the postcapitalist future,* in favor of dividuating transsubjective movements of creative-relational self-decision, carried to their highest power. This is what Nietzsche meant when he spoke of the overcoming of the human by its own more-than-human powers of becoming. It is also what Foucault referred to when he spoke of "Man" as "a face drawn in the sand at the edge of the sea" (Foucault 1994, 387). The "human" and "Man" are the collective categories under which the process of personalization has subsumed its would-be sovereign individuals.

Lemma a. The postcapitalist individual will be processually *more-than-human* and culturally *post-Man.*

SCHOLIUM B. A distinction needs to be made between *personalization* (the proprietary capture of affect toward the constitution of a purportedly sovereign, separable all-too-human subject) and *personification.* A personification is an expression of nonhuman forces. It is a bundling together of a selection of pre-personal tendencies bubbling at the dividual level, bumped up to a higher level in such a way that their composition takes on a rhythm or consistency (but not a self-sufficiency or whole-ness) of expression. "Processual *figure*" is another word for a personification. "Persona" is another. These are really just other names for "subject" in the broad, processual sense discussed above (T53), as grasped from the angle of a consistency of emergent expression. They are surplus-values of expression. The Trump persona is a notable contemporary figure of the capitalist process (T56, T71). There are also precapitalist and—undoubtedly—postcapitalist modes of personification (T69).

SCHOLIUM C. One of the main conduits of the personalizing capture of affect in emotion is *narrative*. Narrative can oper-ate in many modes, to different power effect, and can foster escape (T70). However, there is a complicity between certain modes of deployment of narrative and neoliberalism's person-alization dynamic that make it a central operator of capitalist power's production of well-channeled human capital. For lack of a better term, this mode of narrative deployment can be called "aspirational." Aspirational narrative is what puts the speculative, future-looking aspect fundamental to the defini-tion of capital into the movements of human capital in a way that helps prime those movements for capitalist surplus-value accumulation along well-oiled paths. It does this by equating capitalist surplus-value with *deferred surplus-value of life.* Make yourself competitive on the job market as a versatile entre-preneur of yourself, and reap the benefits later in the form of an affluent quality of life in your middle years (who knows, if you play the field well, you might even be able to retire early; don't neglect your self-funded pension plan). Self-drive and accumulate, at all costs. In the process, tend to yourself. Tend your self, so you don't burn out. Self-help literature and media is the growth market in aspirational narrative. But the aspi-rational mode of generic narrative also ripples across other narrative forms populating the media, from Hollywood into its digital beyond. It is pervasive in marketing, fast becoming through social media a veritable mode of being rather than a separate sphere of activity. Under neoliberalism, the individual has a great degree of autonomy in constructing its own aspirational narratives. Each construction largely falls under the sway of a generic narrative serving as a template. The narrative freedom available to the neoliberal individual is to *appropriate* and *customize* a generic narrative, toward its own human-capitalist *self-molding*. The individual is tasked with continuously folding itself into an aspirational narrative arc, and its arc into its self. When generic narratives are imposed in straight disciplinary manner, as in racial or gender stereotypes, it is experienced as an oppression. By contrast, the aspirational exercise of narrative power is misrecognized as a freedom. The individual expresses its "freedom" by *recognizing itself* in its custom-tailored—"personal"—generic narrative. The aspirational relation of the future to the past is figured as a stepwise becoming *more like oneself.* The master trope, explicitly or implicitly, is *self-actualization.* Self-sameness is projected into the future as the achievement of a continuing labor of therapeutic or self-molding self-recognition. Self-sameness becomes, paradoxically, a matter of becoming. The sense of self-sameness involved is demonstrably fuzzy. Aspirational narratives are always so constructed as to allow a certain drift or lack of focus. Their frequent failure to sharpen into focus or remain on track is not disavowed, but it is not allowed to undermine the sense of self-recognition. After all, self-actualization is a work in progress, and part of what has to be self-lovingly recognized are one's own weaknesses and inconsistencies. This builds a certain plasticity into the sense of self (sameness), not inconsistent with the general operation of channeling the future in capitalist directions. Not only does it form personal life entirely as a future-looking function of surplus-value production, each variant potentially becomes a new generic template, auguring an emergent niche market. The generic arcing toward self-actualization exerts a moderating influence on the self-driving of human capital as it surfs the quasi-chaotic flows of the capitalist field, holding it to forms largely articulable with the archaism-with-a-contemporary function that is liberalism. Classical discipline, illiberal at heart, is much less plastic. It imposes narratives to model the individual in avowedly rigid ways. Although narrative is always a part of how discipline works, it is not the primary mode in which it operates. It employs narrative as means among others, adjutant to its primary mode, which is inculcation according to a model rather than channeling as a function of a deformable generic template. There is always a certain plasticity in narrative, even under a classically disciplinary regime. But in classical discipline, the plasticity is incidental. Under neoliberalism, it is essential and operationalized. Narrative channeling under neoliberalism is by and large an operator of self-acted personalization, conducted with self-referential reverence rather than other-world-directed rectitude: a *piety of the personal* requiring heart and soul participation, but in the form of *buy-in* rather than belief (making it, in effect, a heartfelt *cynicism*). In the final analysis, what is narratively afoot is a plastic form of self-normalization consisting in a quasi-disciplinary channeling hybridized with ontopower. The disciplinary part is that the generic narrative arcs stand as models (self standard). The "quasi-" part is that the models are self-applied and operate as deformable self-moldings (self-channeling). This edges into ontopower, as the whole process gets under the skin of a life's movement, exerting an immanently incitative (aspirational) force of personal ontogenesis, plastically inscribed in the general province of the same (self-becoming). This is the neo/liberal regime of self–soft capture. At its ontopowerful extreme, human capital bursts out of this narrative envelope into a personification of the deregulated flows of capital as such (T56). When it does so, it performatively embraces its dividuality in a quasi-chaotic mode more intensely, and idiosyncratically, expressive of the tenor of the capitalist process as a whole.

Lemma b. An emotion is a *unit of personalizing narrative.* Human capital's generic self-molding is composed of emotional pearls strung together in a self-actualizing necklace circling the person.

SCHOLIUM D. This is not all emotion is. As always, there is an excess-over any capture: a surplus of affect that is fed forward as surplus-value of life, moving the life-process forward. *Emotion is shot through with affect.* It carries intensity. Its narrative development, in all of its modes, is motored by affective intensities, whose lively expression narrative channels into its own proceeding. The unitization of affect as emotion is a narrative *coding* of affect. Affect as such is *neither unitizable nor codable.* It is more-than-narrative. That is why narrative can be escaped—and why escape can be narrative. When narrative fosters escape, it is affectively escaping its own coding. It is overspilling emotion, to rejoin the excess of intensity moving through it.

T68

Being more-than-narrative, affect is *extra-personal.*

T69

A postcapitalist future will have to operate *beyond the personal,* to reclaim affect and intensity, by whatever means necessary.

SCHOLIUM. There may well be different understandings of personhood, constructed according to other principles, for example, along animist principles, as articulated in contemporary anthropology in relation to indigenous cultures (Viveiros de Castro 2014; Kohn 2013). These only exist in a systematic way in noncapitalist societies. However, in a certain way they are very much with us in capitalist culture: as prefigured in forms of escape, ephemeral and precarious, bidding for the noncapitalist future. More sustainable modes of divergent personification—*alter-personhoods*—retaining a certain animism will have to be *invented* for the postcapitalist world. These will be in escape both from the generic narratives of neoliberal personalization and from the more deregulated, less self-integrated, more ontopowerful personifications of capital with which neoliberal personalization coexists and co-operates (T56, T58, T71 Schol. a). Conceptual tools for alternate notions of the person exist within Western culture in the work of C. S. Peirce and A. N. Whitehead. Alter-personhoods are postcapitalist subjects that processually embrace their self-driving subjectivity-without-a-subject to affirm the intensities of surplus-value of life.

> **Lemma.** The capitalist process is as much, if not more, an enterprise of the *production of subjectivity* as it is of the production of goods (Guattari 1995). This is a power that can be turned against it.

T70

The invention of post-capture affective process for the postcapitalist world does not have to dispense with narrative. It can qualitatively convert it, for example by practicing it in the mode of *fabulation*.

> **Scholium.** Fabulation (Manning forthcoming; Deleuze 1989: 126–55; Guattari 2014, 37–38) alters the balance between memory of the past and memory of the future. Aspirational narrative caresses the past with self-love (all the more so if the past were full of self-loathing). Fabulation does not mythologize

the past. It weights narrative away from memory of the past toward memory of the future. This changes the ratio of self-recognition to self-becoming in favor of the latter. It backgrounds self-recognition, subordinating it to the *surprise* of becoming. Fabulation is the resingularization of narrative. The dominant affective tenor shifts from the familiarity of self-sameness to the *wonder* of self-producing creativity. Wonder is the name for emotion's outdoing by affect's opening to creative advance. In the postcapitalist future, as important as the withering of the State will be the *withering of emotion* (that is, the reaffirmation of affective intensities out from under the arc of personalization).

T71

Under neoliberalism the narrative capture of affect is *generally normalizing or singularly pathological—or both at the same time,* in oscillation.

> **Lemma.** It is this oscillation that characterizes neoliberal capitalism as "postnormative" in its overall processual reach.

> **SCHOLIUM A.** The deregulation tendency of neoliberal capitalism extends to the emotional composition of the person. Its subjects' self-fashionings have a tendency to run away with themselves, in spite of their generic narrative channeling. This actually occurs when the grand narrative of "individualism" that is so much a part of neoliberalism (even though its process is always taking away with its invisible subjectivity-without-a-subject hand what its system gives with its more perceptible individualizing handshake) is taken too much to heart. Enabled by the general conditions of plasticity that are a part even of the most generic personalization, hyperindividualism can push beyond the pale to breed downright idiosyncrasies. This can result in hypereffective human-capitalist entrepreneurs of themselves

who capitalize on their borderline abnormality, including some embodying cartoonish exaggerations of generic narrative norms (harvesting internet surplus-value of flow, for example, through their personal YouTube channels). It also breeds monsters, when the individualism gets overly "rugged" (although what passes for ruggedness nowadays seems to be more a severe reactivity: an extreme sensitivity immediately turned around into aggressive backlash against any perceived slight or injury). Donald J. Trump's overbearing glee in his breaking of the norms of good conduct, and his neoliberal embrace of corruption, exemplifies this. The idea of the "good citizen" doesn't even ring a bell for this hypercapitalist. Neither does narrative coherence. Narrative self-actualization is a regime of self-referential truth, that of the subject becoming more like itself. But at the extreme, that becoming rushes headlong, and headstrong, into the borderline world of a "post-truth" regime. Shards of narrative are produced in profusion, always refracted through the distorting prism of a hypermasculinity exaggerating its generic template to absurd dimensions. Emotivity flies off its hinges. The absurdity is such that it is hard to take a figure such as Trump seriously as a person. This is reflected in the colloquial use of his name as a common noun: *the* Donald. Perhaps the Donald embodies a certain, hypercapitalist, overcoming of the person. He is certainly not an emotionally integrated one. Perhaps he embodies an *immanent alter-personhood describing the limit of neoliberal capitalist subjectivity.* If so, even though it takes the personal movement of the process of capitalism down an approach to the limit, it is unlikely to bring the entire process to a tipping point. This is because the hypermasculinism of his persona gestures to generic figures of the masculine, as a condition of its hypering of them. This enables more everyday, less deregulated capitalist subjects *to recognize themselves in him in spite of his excesses* and *in spite of their having no basis for an identification with him*. By what criterion is there a sameness between a billionaire born into wealth and privilege and a middle American in the Rust Belt with the fear of God in them about falling into poverty (if they are not already in it)? Weirdly, Trumpians are *recognizing their own difference* in his distorted mirror. They are seeing what they experience as their own *exceptionalism*: what makes them special as Americans vis-à-vis the hated un-American Americans (that is, their own rugged individualism—or reactivity). The hate list includes "liberal progressives" (who conspiratorially control the "mainstream media" and the "deep state" establishment), immigrant "job-stealers," and "entitled" African Americans. Traditional theories based on identification with a "charismatic leader" (bumbling, orange-tinged, militantly ignorant, gaffe-happy Trump, charismatic?) cannot begin to account for his phenomenon.

SCHOLIUM B. An affective analysis is necessary, which is beyond the scope of the present account. Such an analysis would have to account for the way in which the Donald-person (or persona) is wholly and completely a *media figure*—as *an immediate mode of existence*. What is a media figure in today's field of life? How can it be both a media figure and an immediate mode of existence? A concept of *"immediation"* will have to be developed to bridge this gap (Manning, Thomsen, and Munster forthcoming). The analysis will also have to grapple with the inherent *polyvalence* of the media figure (another reason theories of identification employing a traditional notion of personhood don't work). In this case, that polyvalence manifests in the way in which the Donald's deregulated limit-case person spins off normativity effects among some followers, while replicating its own monstrosity among others: how he kingpins an oscillation between the normative and the pathological (or sociopathic). The normative swing has to do with the way in which the refractions of self-recognition passing through his media figure rebound on and stoke the reaction-formations discussed earlier (T54–T56), in their more traditional religious-right or right-wing conservative versions. The pathological and sociopathic swing has to do with how these same refractions seed neo-reactionary mini-me monsters. It depends on what soil they fall on (how they fall back on the field of emergence, like fungal spores). The analysis of the Donald as affective-refractor mechanism will hinge on the paradox of the *becoming-reactive* of affirmative life forces, in potentially so potent a way as to make a veritable contagion, even of the most extreme versionings; a real viral possibility. In other words, the question of *fascism,* once again, cannot be avoided in any project for the revaluation of values, which can only be predicated on the *affirmative* becoming-more-intensely-active of formative forces.

T72

The creation of postcapitalist alternatives needs to find *creative ways to play the affect/intensity differential* that counter the modes of capture of creative tension that are a part of the contemporary ecology of powers, avoiding in particular the personalizing capture of affect in emotion endemic to the capitalist economization process that goes along with it.

Scholium. Emotion underwrites personalization. Personalization, under neoliberalism, feeds normativity, human-capital self-channeling, and emotive swings toward a postnormative becoming-reactive of affirmative life forces, in strange oscillation and many a proliferating variation (among them, approaches to the limit where personalization approaches verge on and in some cases actually tip over into inhuman—monstrous, sociopathic—personification). Given the potency, polyvalence, and ubiquity of these operations, the merest emotional appeasement of the piety of the personal threatens to derail the deployment of postcapitalist potential.

T73

This is *not to say that depersonalization is the answer.*

SCHOLIUM. Depersonalization is the simple dialectical opposite of personalization. It is itself a kind of reaction-formation. It breeds monsters of its own (tending toward psychosis). It threatens to simply dis-integrate the person. The postcapitalist subject will not be an unintegrated person but a whole new animal. What is needed is an integral alter-formation.

T74

To begin with, what is needed is actually much more modest: an *escape hatch.*

SCHOLIUM. The postcapitalist future will grow in the pores of the capitalist field of life, in much the same way Marx said that capitalist society grew in the pores of feudalism. This resonates with what today is called *prefigurative politics* (the idea that our resistances to capital and power today must endeavor to embody embryonically the qualities that will characterize the postcapitalist future). The immediate task is to craft *temporary autonomous zones* that might release postcapitalist potential into the wild, to proliferate. These are not just vacuoles. They are full of hyperdifferentiation: a plethora of qualitative differentials in creative tension. They are not disorganized, but rather full to overflowing with alter-organization. The concept of alter-economic temporary autonomous zones as connected to the revaluation of values envisioned here is in dialogue with the original term (Bey 2003), but with differences of approach and emphasis, particularly as regards creative duplicity.

T75

To be at all sustainable, even temporarily, the autonomous zones must be able to interface with the existing economy. To do so, they must *practice creative duplicity in relation to quantification and economization.*

SCHOLIUM. Otherwise they will be crushed.

T76

This means that they must play their own differential with capitalist economization. They must be *relationally autonomous* with regards to it: carving out their own eddy of processual singularity, while at the same time coupling processually with capitalism for the time being (until a tipping point is reached).

SCHOLIUM A. Otherwise they will starve.

SCHOLIUM B. In any case, they have no choice in this matter, given that complicity is an ontological condition under neoliberal capitalism (T34 Schol. c, T60). They cannot stake out a position outside the capitalist field, because it only has an *immanent* outside. This in no way means that they will be "all in" it. *There is no position of purity from which to oppose capitalism.* There is no more a being all in, than there is the possibility of stepping outside (T60 Schol. a). There is power in this duplicitous positioning that is potentially creative. There is no reason in principle why creative duplicity cannot immanently *leverage postcapitalist difference.*

SCHOLIUM C. It is not as if *not* exploring an alter-economy interested in, and in creative tension with, the model of financial capital will avoid complicity. All existing alter-economies interface with the dominant economy in one way or another, of necessity, as does every individual involved in them who has ever earned a wage, bought a product, opened a bank account, or benefited from a pension. The ways in which funding is conventionally obtained for collective projects (government grants, foundation grants, crowdfunding) are all deeply complicit with neoliberalism in their own ways, and come with the added disadvantage that the nonprofit status often involved in those efforts requires a legal organizational structure that repeats the basic characteristics of the corporate model (officers, board of directors, membership conceived as shareholding or stakeholding, annual meetings, etc.) and a day-to-day management structure reproducing the conventional hierarchy (at least on paper). Everyone is already practicing creative duplicity, and short of a global revolution will continue to do so. Historically, even the most radical of revolutions have been recuperated by capital. It cannot be assumed that it will be different the next time around—unless the postcapitalist future is already availably prefigured in the interim. So the issue is not whether to practice creative duplicity, but which complicit duplicities and in what way. There is no a priori reason not to explore all avenues, even the ones that the left traditionally holds under the highest suspicion. Striking a posture of purity will get nowhere. It too easily absolves one of engaging, day to day, hour by hour, with the real conditions of life, as part of an ongoing struggle reaching down to the microlevels of existence. Sustained engagement of that kind is necessary if those conditions are to be sustainably changed. "Certainly now is the time to create money designed to stoke demand for new financial tools for activists, collectives, social movements, artists, refugees, and all who struggle for a life worth living so that they might catch and keep their own value for themselves" (Beller 2017, 10).

T77

A promising lead toward constructing an escape hatch that avoids the emotional-personal capture of neoliberal capitalism, while creatively playing the affect/intensity differential in ways that processually couple with economization, but still prefiguring a postcaptalist future, carrying rewilding potential, and leveraging postcapitalist difference, might be found in the notion of *intensive magnitude*.

> **Lemma a.** Exploring intensive magnitude in a postcapitalist perspective requires introducing *aesthetic categories* into political economy.

> **Lemma b.** This involves rethinking *causality*.

SCHOLIUM A. Intensity has two imbricated aspects or dimensions, qualitative and quantitative, whose differential has been a continuing concern of these theses because it lies at the heart of economization. We place ourselves in different dimensions of the same event depending on whether we approach it from the causal point of view, or whether we consider it as "self-sufficing" (Bergson 2001, 90, 137). To underline that "causal" is not necessarily a linear concept, the word "*conditioning*" is a better choice. "Conditioning" extends to emergent effects (event-derivatives) of a qualitative order that are not reducible to the sum of their parts, and whose emergence is integrally relational rather than owing to a linear transmission of force. There is always a quantitative dimension to the conditioning of events, imbricated with qualitative dimensions. The nature of that imbrication must be taken into account. For example, pain, as we experience it, is self-sufficing: it directly expresses itself for what it is, just as it is, needing nothing other than itself to explain what it is and to make a definite difference in our lives. It is a *pure quality* (Bergson 2001, 90): an immediate experiential life-quality. It is "pure" in the sense that it is irreducible to any quantification of its conditioning factors. "Reducing all qualities to quantities is absurd" (Nietzsche 2003, 91–92). The quality, self-sufficing, is supernumerary. But this does not mean that it can be understood without reference to quantity. The affect of pain is greater when its conditioning factors include a greater number of physical disturbances, meaning that the tissue damage is more *extensive* (Bergson 2001, 34). The number of the disturbances does not express itself directly in the felt *intensity* of the pain. The disturbances express themselves not quantitatively, but as a greater degree of the same quality. By degree of quality is meant its *insistency*: a greater degree of pain insists more on its own quality. It claims more emphasis for that quality, and backgrounds other concurrent qualities of experience behind the cry of its own expression. Insistency is a question of *qualitative emphasis*. A lesser pain is not less qualitative: it is more insistently purely qualitative. Its qualitative intensity, it is true, rises and falls in lockstep with the number of factors involved. But "as soon as we try to measure it, we unwittingly replace it by space" (Bergson 2001, 106). The intensity of a pain, for example, might be associated with a more extensive array of organic disturbances, or a stronger localization of its cause. Measure translates the intensity of the quality into spatial extension—which, of course, it cannot in actuality come without, even if, in the event, it cannot be reduced to it. When we measure, we are toggling between two necessary dimensions, intensity and extension, that are mutually enveloped in the event. Measure is a technique for treating those dimensions as separable. Separating the dimensions *takes the intensity out of the event*. Its extensive aspect is measured, and the numbers thus *extracted* from the event are moved into another event-domain, where they function as indexes of the event and its inherent intensity.

SCHOLIUM B. Another example makes the processual imbrication of quality and quantity more intuitive. Take two flocks of starlings on two consecutive days. On the first day, there are ten. The second day, after a major migratory influx, there are ten thousand. Now imagine a startle that flushes the starlings into flight. Think of the quality of the movement in each case. The ten thousand bank and turn, folding into and through each other with wondrous grace and beauty, thickening into swirling creases and thinning out into scatter zones, the swirling and scattering themselves folding into and out of each other with awe-inspiring topological complexity. All of this is measurable. But it would be a defiance to even try to speak of the event without employing *aesthetic* terms. These starlings have *zest*. The measure of their movements would miss the *eventness* of the event: its singular quality that makes it stand out as an event, backgrounding for an instant everything else. The eventness of the event is a pure quality. Now think of the ten taking flight. This is still impressive, for a landlubber species such as ours. But it is impressive in a comparatively measly way. It is not awe inspiring and does not bring words like "wondrous grace and beauty" to the tips of our tongues. This congregation of birds has less zest. The movement is qualitatively different, carrying less topological *potential* owing to the smaller number of contributory starling factors. The movement has its own quality, just of lesser intensity. Both takings-flight involve a number of birds. The number of birds in each case corresponds to a greater or lesser occupation of sky space. But this extensive element does not come without being *enveloped in a qualitative difference* that insists on itself, in an irreducibly *aesthetic manner*. The quality of the events are conditioned by the quantities involved, without being reducible to them.

SCHOLIUM C. In this example, the greater number corresponded to the greater intensity. This is generally but not necessarily the case. Intensity fundamentally has to do with the qualitative range of the potential enveloped, and its ability to insist on itself: to make itself *presently palpable.* A small number of elements may mutually cohere in movement in a way that envelops a greater intensity of potential than a larger number of the same kind of elements, depending on the nature of the elements and the manner of their concertation. This is due to the fact that the *contributory subtendencies insist on themselves,* as well as their integral expression insisting on itself, and the quality of the global expression is modulated as a function of that. To return to the pain example, it is well known that anxious tensing increases the intensity of pain, and that the cultivation of certain "mindful" countertendencies of attention decreases it. These techniques reach down to the subtendency level. *The relation between extension and intensity is not linear.* Tendencies go all the way down qualitatively, and their differentials make a difference at every level.

> **Lemma c.** The term *intensive magnitude* highlights the way each event comprises a quantitative aspect (expressing itself in the extensive dimension of space) and a qualitative dimension (expressing itself in the aesthetic dimension of a purely qualitative difference of degree).

> **Lemma d.** Placed in contrast to intensive magnitude, *affective intensity* tips toward the qualitative difference of degree comprising the aesthetic dimension (bearing in mind the intentional range of ambiguity encompassed in this and allied terms, as discussed in T43 Schol. c).

SCHOLIUM D. It is important not to forget the complexities of the vocabulary around affect and intensity, and to keep sight of the role of qualitative differentials (in the starling example, the differentials of flying *style* between the individual birds in the flock, as indexed by variations in speed, acceleration, and spacing between bodies, composing the flock's overall manner of flying). In the light of the contrast between intensive magnitude and affective intensity, *intensity* can be used as a shorthand for affective intensity, since the term "intensive magnitude" takes on the role it can otherwise have of referring to the way the quantitative and the qualitative have of coming together.

Lemma e. The *conditions* of the event are struck by the same two-sidedness as the event itself.

SCHOLIUM E. When we refer to conditioning elements or contributory factors, there is always the dual aspect of the qualitative differentials in their aesthetic dimension (style, manner) and the quantifiable differentials (bearing on the extensive factors of number, speed, spacing, size). This can be prized apart if need be.

Lemma f. This is because the event is composed of subevents. *Eventness goes "all the way down."*

Lemma g. An aesthetic way of referring to intensive magnitude is to use the term *zest* (Whitehead 1967, 258).

Lemma h. Zest is another word for vitality affect. Zest registers *adventure* (Whitehead 1967, 299, 304).

Lemma i. The corresponding aesthetic term for the pure quality of the event, considered in abstraction from its zestiness, is *beauty* (Whitehead 1967, 252–72). Beauty is affective intensity, as it verges on emotion.

Lemma j. Wonder is the affective outdoing of beauty.

SCHOLIUM F. Wonder peaks with the event's culmination, whereas zest and adventure are integrally bound up with its unfolding. Beauty, for its part, abstracts from the event as if it were in suspense (without going so far as to separate it from its intensity). Zest, beauty, wonder, and adventure provide aesthetic categories that might pave the way for the revaluation of values to go beyond normative criteria and judgment. These are *felt qualities*, not rationalities or ratiocinations. They provide purely qualitative indexes for the intensive power of becoming expressing itself in the self-forming of events. No account of value can do without criteria of *evaluation*. These terms provide elements of a vocabulary for the evaluation of the *quality of the process* coming to expression. They cannot be understood as "merely" subjective (as individual and personal). They must be recognized as transindividual: as indexing the more-than-humanness of the process's self-driving. Not being categories of judgment, they cannot be mistaken for *taste*, or personal preference. That they are felt qualities means that if they could be construed as judgments, they would have to be *lived judgments* (abductions). They come in the thick of things: unmediated. Lived judgments can only be evaluated participatorily and *experimentally*. Like all qualities, they are such as they are. They cannot be second-guessed. They happen as they happen, or they don't. If they do, they make a *pragmatic* difference in the subsequent quality of the process as it turns over on itself for another run. Instead of being rationally judged, they must be *improvised* flush with events. They are a *project*, not a grid of analysis. Without a concerted tendential direction—also immanent to the unfolding—they are liable to run out of steam, or run afoul of themselves. The contrast discussed earlier between the bullying becoming-reactive of formative forces and their affirmative becoming-active provides a qualitative criterion for the immanent evaluation of tendential direction. Together, these go some way toward a nonnormative *ethico-aesthetics* for the revaluation of values (Massumi 2017b).

T78

Politically and economically, the reason to go through these intensive maneuvers is to hold fast to the fact that *affective intensity is inextricably linked to potential,* and that this connection is key to the revaluation of values.

> SCHOLIUM A. "The affective state must correspond not merely to the physical disturbances, movements or phenomena which have taken place, but also, and especially, to *those which are in preparation, those which would like to be"* (Bergson 2001, 34; translation modified, emphasis added). In other words, enveloped in the quality of the event is an excess of unactualized potentials, movements that were preparing themselves to occur, were pressing to be carried out, that would have "liked to be" (little wills to ontopower), but didn't end up making it into the event's actual composition. Their pressing and preparing is part of the insistence of the event, even if many of the pressing potentials do not *actually* take part in its completion. It is the expressed quality of the intensive envelopment of these pressing potentials that distinguishes this co-motion of tendencies from the quantitative and extensive side of the event. In the starling example, each bird at every moment had to be poised for a nearly instantaneous tack or swerve. When there are ten birds, the quality of the movement is more regular and less particular, so the potential moves that must be in preparation (in preacceleration) at each instant are fewer. This is reflected in each individual's flying style, and simultaneously in the mannerism of the flock. In the flock of ten thousand, each bird has to be braced for quicker and more variable movements. They cannot not feel this, flush with their movements. The feeling shades off into the field of emergence, to a level where the qualitative differentials between the movements an individual bird

is poised for shade off into infinitesimal contrasts between potential movements. At this level of bare activity (T46 Schol. a),
each bird is braced into a heightened state of affective intensity,
immanent to the event. Each embodies a quantum of the event's
dipping down to the infinitesimal level of its field of emergence.
Each individual expresses the global intensity of the event to a
degree corresponding to the comprehensiveness of its dipping
to the infinitesimal level of potential (depending on its skill,
the alacrity of its reflexes, its individual physiological traits,
and its health). It is not only that the overall movement of the
smaller flock is less intense: *the qualitative difference in degree
of intensity also goes all the way down, to the level of in-braced
potential* (the immanent outside). It is the *manner* in which it
goes all the way down that correlates with the event's intensive
magnitude, regardless of the number of elements in play.

SCHOLIUM B. This in-bracing makes all the difference. But the
difference it makes cannot be measured, even if the individuals composing the event can be counted. At the infinitesimal
level of in-braced potential, incoming into the event, the contrasts between potential movements enter a *zone of indistinction* where no sooner does one begin to sketch itself than it
turns over into another, then that one into yet another, in the
churning of potential that is bare activity. The bare activity of
the zone of indistinction describes the *immanent limit* of the
field of emergence. At the limit, it zones into the virtual. This
immanent co-motion roils into the continuing of the collective
movement, as the pressing of the potentials tumbles over each
individual move, and rolls over from one move to the next to
globally compose the collective movement. This is the by-now-
familiar movement of surplus-value production. The *in-bracing
drives the surplus-value of life of the event* (which in this case is

also an instance of surplus-value of motion). The rolling over of the surplus-value of the event dynamically fuses the multiplicity of contributing factors into the singular continuing of the event: it produces the event as a continuum. Surplus-value is the *power of the continuum*. Financial derivatives, in their tendential convergence between quality and quantity (T46), effect the capitalist approach to the power of the continuum, toward the appropriation of that power for capitalist surplus-value production. An unappropriable postcapitalist version of the same convergence must be invented for alter-economic purposes.

> **Lemma a.** Politically and economically, the notion of the fusional imbrication of multiplicity in the continuum of the event is important because the continuum is the event's *transindividuality* (its continuing integrally across its individual factors) and because that transindividuality isn't a thing but a *power*. It is the power of becoming of a subjectivity-without-a subject.

> **SCHOLIUM C.** "When the continuum is the trace of a motion, the associated infinitesimal/intensive magnitudes have been identified as *potential* magnitudes—entities that, while *not possessing true magnitude themselves,* possess a *tendency* to generate magnitude through motion, so manifesting 'becoming' as opposed to 'being'" (Bell 2013; emphasis added).

> **Lemma b.** Power cannot fully be understood without making qualitative reference to tendency as play of potential.

T79

Power cannot *be reduced to the actual exercise of force,* if force is understood as necessarily having magnitude. Tendencies are qualitative forces of event-formation. They are *qualitative formative forces.*

SCHOLIUM A. The qualitative goes all the way down, until it melds with event-potential. Event-potential is *supernumerary*: it is of the nature of surplus-value. It is also *superqualitative*: packing together an ultimately indistinct multiplicity of qualitative differentials in a way that does erase them. Because they are not erased, each roil and tumble integrally reshuffles the field, shaking out a certain differential spread of potentials that rise back up toward the surface of the event, where they are more distinctly felt, press harder, and thus become more accessible for actualization. *There is no bedrock quantitative level* from which quality emerges. The "bedrock" is the churning sea of immanent potential that is the field of life as bare activity, from which the two streams of the quantitative and qualitative spill: a potential cannot actualize without taking on extension and magnitude, but each move, each actualization, also spins off pure quality, affectively enveloping intensity. In the actualization of the event, quantity and quality are two sides of the event at every level, all the while remaining distinct event-dimensions. The qualitative on one level coils up into and is boosted onto the next. The qualitative snakes up the levels climbing the steps of its own event-dimension, culminating in the global affect expressing the quality of the event as a whole (the feeling of a degree of temperature, or the beauty of the overall topological figure of the flock of starlings). Likewise for quantity, culminating in a numerical extraction. Quality snakes with quality, and quantity with quantity. *Neither "causes" the other.* Neither is epiphenomenal. One is not more real than the other. They are really different, aboriginal dimensions of the same event-conditioning. They co-condition the event. They *do not mix,* and yet their emergent effects *fuse* into the singularity of the event's taking off. A suggestive image for this is the *caduceus* (the staff used as a symbol of the medical profession): two intercoiled snakes that do not touch, yet nevertheless rise up to take wing together.

SCHOLIUM B. "The fact is that there is no point of contact between the unextended and the extended, between quality and quantity. We can interpret the one by the other, set up the one as the equivalent of the other; but sooner or later, at the beginning or at the end, we shall have to recognize the conventional character of this assimilation" (Bergson 2001, 70).

> **Lemma.** The potential in-braced into the event qualitatively *underwrites intensity,* in the currency of experience. The systematic extraction of number from the quantitative dimensions *overwrites* it, in the conventional coinages of science.

T80

Even though neither quantity nor quality are epiphenomenal, neither is more real than the other, and they come together in the event—still, *quality is processually primary in relation to quantity.*

SCHOLIUM A. Quality recoils into the immanence of potential underwriting the process. At this level, event-factors no longer count themselves out. They brace themselves in. They brace into the event, and into each other's proximity. They move together to the limit where they enter a zone of indistinction composing a continuum whose power is beyond number. It is precisely because quality is primary in relation to quantity that potential must be *captured* and channeled by systems of quantification—prime among them capitalist economization.

SCHOLIUM B. The intensive excess of the qualitative over the quantitative never balances out. There is an *essential asymmetry.* Otherwise, process could fall into equilibrium. It would suffer from the *entropy* native to extensive, spatialized systems.

There is a creative advance of process precisely because there is a countervailing tendency to entropy: a *negentropy*. This countervailing is the *tendency of tendency* to continuously "generate [intensive] magnitude through motion." Think again of the heightened relational sensitivity of the individual starlings' movements in the flock of ten thousand, and the way it packs potential into the flocking-event's global motion, intensely *animating the number* of starlings. Qualitative differential is the animating force; quantification piggybacks the entropic force.

T81

The inextricability of affective intensity and potential *in-forms* the event with a *variety of tendencies,* only some of which actually play out.

> SCHOLIUM A. "*Variety*" is a word for the qualitative dimension of a multiplicity. It denotes a differential field of qualitatively different tendencies (secondarily, it connotes a number spread, a plurality of kinds distributed in space, into which that field extensively folds out).

> SCHOLIUM B. As the variety of the tendencies churns through the continuity of the event, their differentials play out into a singular affective expression: that of the global quality marking the culmination of the event. The global quality is the qualitative summing-up of the qualitative recoils leveling up into it, and at the same time descending to the immanent outside where they dip into potential, in event-powering *rhythmic* turnover. That rhythm is the immanent dynamic form (the self-in-forming) of the event. It is the dynamic form of a subjectivity-without-a-subject. A system's processual turnover (T16) follows the rhythm.

T82

The rhythmic playing out of the in-forming tendencies constitutes a *power of becoming,* as opposed to being, that is not reducible to actual exercises of force. It is a life-driving *force-beyond-force.*

T83

Number, extracted, indexes quality. *Quality, in-formed, indexes potential.*

T84

This cross-indexing of quantity, quality, and potential, implicit in the concept of intensive magnitude, *enables the force-beyond-force of the power of becoming to be mobilized.*

> **Lemma a.** This mobilization of the power of becoming is synonymous with *ontopower.*

> **Lemma b.** Since the power of becoming is the power of the continuum, *the mobilization must ultimately be of variety,* of qualitative differentials. It must mobilize them in transindividual fashion, bearing directly on the dynamic fusion of the event. It must be *transversal,* concerned with the way in which the excess of potential *carries across* the individual contributing factors, to recoil up and down the levels composing the intensive magnitude, in a rhythm of dynamic fusion.

T85

It is conceivable that the force-beyond-force of the power of becoming (ontopower) can be mobilized in a way that makes possible an *alter-economization* that does not subsume surplus-value of life / surplus-value of flow under capitalist surplus-value.

> **Scholium a.** Were this to be achieved, economization would

be in the service of life-driving powers of becoming, rather than life-driving powers of becoming being in the service of accumulation.

Lemma. This would qualify the alter-economization as a *counter-ontopower.*

Scholium b. The fact that that power is not reducible to the exercise of force—that there is a force-beyond-force that can be alter-economized as a counter-ontopower—is critical to the revaluation of values: it points to the potential *power of non-violence* (T99).

T86

In a counter-powerful alter-economy, surplus-value of life would retain its value for itself. *Value would be revalued* by the counter-subsumption of traditional (separative/applicative) systems of quantification under life-qualities, the latter affirmed for their pure experiential quality and for the in-formative role they play in the self-driving of life's creative advance.

Scholium. This would *capitalize on the primacy of the qualitative* over the quantitative (T80), taking it back from its systematic captures: unchanneling it from them. This is the very meaning of the *revaluation of values.*

T87

Such a contrivance would constitute a *creative process engine* theoretically capable of *sustaining itself economically.*

T88

In order to fully avail itself of the potentials afield in today's digital world, this invention of a creative process engine would involve a new kind of *digital platform.*

SCHOLIUM. The potential afield in today's digital world pivots on the internet's powers of nonlocal contagion and amplification, which can intensify powers of becoming stirring in the pores of the capitalist field. This can be for better or for worse (the alt-right). The inclusion in the toolbox of alter-economic counter-ontopower of digital platforms must be carried out with utmost care, and for nontechnical (qualitative, ethico-aesthetic) reasons, rather than out of any technological messianism, fascination with gadgetry, or reflex fallback to a default position. Exploring a technological avenue is a fraught proposition, but it would be simply foolish (an archaism without a contemporary function) to ignore the potential in the name of "real" sociality. Real sociality is as well-founded a concept as the "real" economy.

Lemma. New systems evolving out of the blockchain, *beyond Bitcoin and Ethereum,* could provide a propitious digital environment for alter-economic experimentation.

T89

This vector of digital plaform design would have to be carried out with utmost care, because certain regressive tendencies, of an *anarcho-libertarian* cast, were designed into the original blockchain concept. These tendencies have to be counteracted.

SCHOLIUM. Ideologically, the development of the blockchain was closely associated with libertarian market fundamentalism (Golumbia 2016). Not only is the conventional threefold definition of money uncritically assumed, underplaying the speculative side of cryptocurrencies (T23), it is further assumed that economic activity comes in discrete units of action. Each such unit is a *transaction* between two individuals. The transaction is entered into according to each individual's calculus of its own self-interest. The freeing of the market from the control of the banks and national governments is thus little more than a transactionalist (Iaconesi 2017) *liberation of self-interest*. The blockchain is a technical distillation of the ideology of individual self-interest that is one of the major tendencies in-forming capitalism. It takes capitalism's basic market ideology and tries to purify it, and objectify that purification in a technical system. It radically reinforces the concept of the market that is at the heart of capitalism, along with the *transactional exchange* model that is central to the concept of the market.

Lemma. Anarcho-libertarianism is *anarcho-capitalism*.

T90

Next-generation blockchain-inspired platforms use *smart contracts* to expand the notion of what a transaction can be in ways that may be able to begin to counteract the libertarianism built into blockchain.

SCHOLIUM A. An example is the conjoint "Gravity" and "Space" cryptocurrency platforms under development by the Economic Space Agency (www.esca.io). The idea is that instead of blockchaining simple exchange transactions, transactions can be made programmable and thus infinitely customizable, extending to anything that could be conceived of as a contract. "Contract" is taken in its broadest and most basic definition, as a *conditional engagement* where one action (or set of actions) calls for a return action, either immediately or within a designated time interval. This need not involve an exchange per se, i.e., the use of a currency as medium of exchange and general equivalent. Any proposition for an if–then call and response between actions could be programmed. The actions also need not be individual. For example, a smart contract could specify a set of actions needed to prepare a collective project for taking a step forward in its process, and what will happen when those conditions come together. A simple example would be a collaborative film production, where smart contracts could be used to bring equipment, skills, and resources together for a shoot or a promotional campaign, and once the conditions are in place, trigger these logistical operations into action. They could also be used to organize collaborative input into the creative process of the film's conception. Even more, smart contracts could be used to decentralize decision-making by enabling propositions to be made and voted upon according to pre-agreed-upon protocols. *Logistics, creative collaboration, governance, and the production of value* would then be intertwined through a single platform whose running would be autonomous and distributed, dispensing with the need for an executive hierarchy overhanging the process and lording over its participants. In this way, a certain *commons* of productive activity would be created, with an ethos of collective collaboration and a certain instantiation of direct democracy. The overall system is designed to be customizable down to the lowest level, so that unlike Bitcoin or Ethereum, projects can program a dedicated domain of operations embodying their particular orientations and priorities while at the same time remaining interoperable with the general cryptocurrency environment. With this, the DAO (distributed autonomous organization) evolves into the DPO (distributed programmable organization). With that evolution, the blockchain will have to give way to a more rhizomatic architecture, one that can potentially dispense with the vocabulary of the contract altogether. Holochain provides a promising example (https://holochain.org; https://blog.p2pfoundation.net/difference-blockchain-holochain/2017/11/02).

SCHOLIUM B. The film production example shows significant

progress in overcoming the individualism of first-generation blockchain. At the same time, the limits of it are easy to see. As soon as there is a *product,* self-interest comes back into the picture. The film will be marketed and make money in the dominant economy. Each individual collaborating on the project will expect a *share* of the profit generated. This is still a capitalist project. The production is market oriented and is aiming for the generation of profit that, in the name of fairness, would have to accrue to the members of the collective according to a pre-agreed protocol (also formalized in a smart contract). The lure of profit is a powerful *attractor.* It is a way of *incentivizing* that activates a plethora of ingrained capitalist—and tendentially individualist—attitudes and habits that could not fail to inflect what creative directions are taken, what propositions are made, and what decisions pass the vote. The creative film process would not be fulfilling itself only for the surplus-value of life it brought to the collaborators and the eventual viewers of the field. It will not be lived and enjoyed purely qualitatively, as a value in itself. In addition to producing surplus-value of life, it will also be lived for quantitative gain, and these two contrasting tendential movements might enter into potentially uncreative tension. The interference between the profit motive and the creative impetus, between collaborative energies and individual gain, would likely *de-intensify* the creative process by making its self-driving be driven by an outside goal.

T91

It may be possible for *tokens* to be used to expand cryptocurrencies beyond the conventional, individual, market-fundamentalist, transaction-based functions of money.

SCHOLIUM A. For example, instead of predesignating a certain share of the profit for each individual, individuals' activity of creating and fulfilling smart contracts could be tracked by an accounting smart contract that allocates tokens based on how much someone contributes. The tokens could be in a crypto-currency that interfaces with Bitcoin or national currencies, so that it could be cashed out. This could conceivably function even in the absence of a saleable end product. That would be possible if the cryptocurrency had a recognized value on the speculative cryptocurrency market, underwritten, as all curren-cies are ultimately in any case, by investor confidence. In other words, it would be backed by *affect* more than by a product-linked tie-in to the "real" economy. This would gain the collec-tive practice a certain autonomy from the capitalist teleology of the marketable product, but would wed it to the speculative logic of the financial market, in its cryptocurrency incarnation, with all of the volatility that comes along with surplus-value of flow and its tendential levitation from the productive econ-omy. The interference between incentivization by individual gain and the collaborative production of surplus-values of life would continue to be a factor. Tokens could also be used in-ternally to the collaborative platform. They could be amassed and then "invested" in decisions. Propositions garnering the greatest number of tokens would get the go-ahead. This has two drawbacks. First, it sneaks back in the equation between *labor-time and monetary value* that lies at the basis of the cap-italist exploitation of live activity: the reward of tokens would correlate to the quantity of input actions, which would in turn correlate to the amount of time invested in them. Secondly, it would reintroduce structural inequality by channeling this capture of life-time into a re-hierarchization of the decision-making playing field. By putting your tokens on the table, you would essentially be buying unequal decision-making power with the capture of your contributed vitality.

Lemma. If it is possible for tokens to be used to expand cryptocurrencies beyond the conventional, individual, market-fundamentalist, transaction-based functions of money, this is something that is *yet to be invented* and will require a great deal of craftiness.

SCHOLIUM B. Alternative token strategies also tend to operationalize a form of value that has not been mentioned up to now, but is fundamental to capitalism: *use-value.* The praise of use-value is often sung in alter-economy communities as a way out of capitalism. This is dangerously naïve. Use-value, it is true, is qualitative: "it is conditioned by the physical properties of the commodity, and has no existence apart from it" (Marx 1976, 126). However, use-value only functions economically to the extent that it "metabolizes" as (is processually converted into) *exchange-value* (Marx 1976, 196–97). The threefold definition of money, and the correlation between quantity of labor-time and quantity of value, are complicit with use-value to the extent that it metabolizes as an economic factor. Measures may be taken to prevent use-value from fully metabolizing with exchange-value (as in skill-sharing networks and other sharing economies; T25). But nothing can prevent it from being haunted by money, the market, and the essentially extortionist correlation between labor-time and value. These slip back in in informal assessments of how "equal" or "fair" a sharing exchange had been, even if such assessment is discouraged. In addition, use-value is *essentially normative.* It is bound up with already-formed *functions* having *conventional values* in one or another systemic context (related to technical systems, productive industries, service industries, or cultural industries, with the definition of "use" varying by domain). By virtue of this systems-participation, a formed function carries a certain *regulatory force,* even outside its dedicated functional context, and in spite of the best efforts to break that link to power. How could the judgment of *usefulness* not carry such a force? All of this is part and parcel of the *work paradigm* so integral to capitalism (even where it is not in force in a full-fledged way as a work ethic). Tokens could theoretically be used in entirely different ways, potentially skirting around use-value, by adopting *gaming* models. However, gaming typically privileges a stimulus–response structure (as opposed to a creative call-and-response process) that re-performs the dominant economy's individual transaction-exchange paradigm, even as it repurposes it for the production of a certain surplus-value of life: *fun.* Fun is a kind of surplus-value of life that is well-known to neoliberal capitalism and well-articulated with it, even to the point of fulfilling a regulatory function in the life of human capital (spawning whole industries: the entertainment sector).

T92

The postblockchain cryptocurrency digital-platform route offers many avenues of response to the capitalist market, but the models now existing or under development so far are stuck in a game of whack-a-mole with it. With every blow against it in one place, the familiar myopic face of one of its constitutive principles *pops up somewhere else.*

T93

Although all manner of commons-centered, collective, collaborative models should be exploratorily pursued and concertedly experimented with, there is a need for projects attempting to go beyond the pale, to cross over today's anarcho-libertarian horizon to new *anarcho-communist* vistas more intensely prefiguring the postcapitalist future.

Scholium. Only a project that operates, in its own processual arena, according to radically anarcho-communist, as opposed to anarcho-capitalist, principles has a chance of beginning to move beyond capitalist economization—and its attendant power formations—in a way that is maximally resistant to re-capture. Intentional communities and autonomous enclaves are a traditional route for experimentation of this kind. Their limitation is that they are obliged for their survival either to opt out of the economy in a way that is rarely sustainable long term, or find ways to link back in through participation in the local economy or the creation of microbusinesses. They also tend to devalue processual excess, which expresses itself most intensely in surplus-value of flow, in favor of a regained rooted-ness in a regulatory ideal of "real life." Their affective intensities often pool around figures of purist return: to "nature," to "au-thenticity," to true "community," and to true activity (craft)—normative notions, all. Experimentation with alter-economic models employing digital currencies can potentially pioneer more sustainable and flexible ecological models, proudly im-pure and without return. Intentional communities and auton-omous enclaves are a welcome element in an alter-economic ecology, as long as they are able to reconcile their dedication to local structure with open system. But they do not provide a general model for alter-economy.

T94

The invention of an anarcho-communist alter-economy would not only have to *eschew the market* as an organizing principle but conscientiously build in mechanisms to *actively ward away* the return of its constitutive tendencies.

Fabulation. Warding-away is a practice of conditioning (very different from causing, structuring, or systematizing; T77

Schol. a). The list of necessary wardings-away is forbidding—or inspiring—depending on how you look at it. They are inspiring if they go hand-in-hand with a constructive set of speculative strategies for building an alter-economy. The strategies would bear on how conditions might be set in place that not only foster a creatively self-driving collective process but also imbue that process with immanently lived criteria, so that a participatory evaluation of the two aspects of the ethico- and the -aesthetic is performed flush with the self-running. The lived criteria, once again, are transindividual intensity and the processual quality of the process's tendential direction. The conditioning strategies weave together into a *speculative fabulation* (T70) of what a collectivist postcapitalist economy might involve. They are fabulatory techniques of relation: a speculative-pragmatic "pseudo-narrative" (Guattari 2014, 37–38). In exceedingly cursory sketch form:

Speculative strategy a. Use-value. The concept of function needs to be replaced with the more plastic concept of operation, making clear that the *operativity* is *processual*. That means that the system remains constitutively open to emergent potential, in-formed by the differential play of tendencies. This involves *operationalizing the immanent outside.*

Speculative strategy b. Fun and games. The differential play of tendencies should be just that: *play.* Gaming models might enter into the larger field of play, especially if they privilege collective action rather than revolving around individual inputs. But they would not define the relational space overall. Play is a more encompassing concept than gaming. Play can take up into itself a heterogeneity of affective intensities. These are *really produced* through the artifice of "make-believe." However, they are produced in an arena where the normative contexts in which they are conventionally found are under suspension (Massumi

2014c), so that the affective intensities are staged independently of their capture by function (playing pirates, for example, does not involve being at sea or making someone actually walk the gangplank—but the players have to *feel* that this is being done). This skirting around use-value allows the unfolding of the intensities to undergo emergent modulation. Play is an operative tendency connoting a processual openness. Events "play out" as their constitutive tendencies unfold. Systems have "play" as they test their limits. Techniques of play-relation are a serious domain for the exploration of alter-unfoldings. These may be staged in such as way as to carry an *exemplary force* for export to extra-play contexts, introducing a margin of play into them that allows them to test their tendential limits. Don't make political platforms. Make play political. Make-believe, but not in the ideological sense of imposing adherence to a program.

Speculative strategy c. Work. The assumption that participation is work would be displaced by building in interactions that have an *improvisational* edge to them. Having an improvisational edge is what defines play. Play should not be confined to any already-recognized arena conventionally designated as a play space within the existing norms of society. Play deploys to intensest effect in temporary autonomous zones. In addition to the multiplicity of affective intensities produced as it unfolds, participation in an improvisational interaction creates a global surplus-value of life that is lived qualitatively as a value, and comprises such sub-surplus-values as zest, beauty, wonder, and adventure. These are expressions of Spinozist *joy.* They accompany the becoming-more-intensely-affirmative of life-formative forces. For Whitehead, the intensity of becoming—"adventure toward novelty"—is the highest "civilizational" value (taking the word "civilization" with a large grain of twenty-first-century salt; Whitehead 1967, viii). To the extent that the collective production of improvised surplus-values of life self-drives an alter-economy, those surplus-values might be called, tongue firmly in cheek, *adventure capital*. Adventure capital, having to do as it does with the affirmation of a life-quality, is a directly aesthetic form of value.

Speculative strategy d. Labor-time. No correlation would be built in, or be allowed to develop, between input of time and production of value. In the postcapitalist future, *time is not money*. It is life. The best way of warding away the time = money equation is to keep the sense of value focused on emergent effects that add up to more than the sum of their parts and that are valued, in the currency of direct experience, for their *incommensurability* with their causal input or conditioning factors. This leveraging of emergent effects is precisely what is meant by improvisation. Improvisation is another word for *free action*: life-activity unsubsumed by the use-value of existing systematic functionings and the work model that goes along with them. The techniques of relation fostering free action combine for a *pragmatics of the useless*. The useless is pragmatic in that it may prefigure the invention of new operations, from which new functions might emerge that were unthinkable within the terms of existing systems.

Speculative strategy e. Individualism. Internal to the project, there would be no division into individual *shares*. This means that on the inside there would be no *unitization* of value, in terms of currency or other forms of tokens. This is done to safeguard improvisation, which is *never a question of individual creativity*. It is always a playing out of a differential field. The field includes suprapersonal factors—habitus, collective memory, cultural allusions, genres, genders, plus any number of nonhuman factors that prime the field and can serve as cues or contingent triggers—as well as infrapersonal factors (the dividual). The latter pertain to the co-motion of bare-active tendencies vying to take hold of the body as a vehicle of their own expression, and to increase their power to self-perform by composing with other tendencies, differentially affecting more than one body in concert through an emergent *collective attunement* to the stirring tendential potential. Improvisation, looked at in this way, is a transindividual machinic subjectivity, or subjectivity-without-a-subject. It operates by synergy and the fusion of a multiplicity of moves into the continuity of a transition. It expresses itself in and as an *emergent collectivity* marshaling the power of a continuum whose fusional taking-form cannot be reduced to the sum of its participating individuals.

Speculative strategy f. Product. No product separate from the process would guide the process teleologically. Emergent collectivity would be valued *as* the product. By emergent is meant that its taking-form is an *event*-form. This would be an *occurrent value*. The events might answer to any number of already-existing arenas, with which they link transversally, resonate at a distance with, or which they parasitize. Art, education, and activism are the key examples. Products might well be produced—artworks, films, books, participatory learning platforms, aesthetico-political activist interventions—but they would not be treated as *the* product. The product would be the continuing of the creative process. Any products other than the self-driving of the creative process engine would be experienced as happy incidentals. A directly collective product of the highest importance would be the spinning-off, from the self-formative movement of the process itself, of *exemplary techniques of relation*. These would be ways of conditioning, triggering, and sustaining emergent collectivity. Techniques of relation would be stored as *process seeds* that could be replanted to move the process through another iteration. They could also be gifted to other collective processes. Their collection would be the only *store of value* that would animate the process. It would amount to a *store of potential.* The techniques would be at the same time *action traces* of past events and *forerunners* (preaccelerators) of future creative variations on them. They would be a qualitative index of the power of the process to turn itself over into its own continuance. In other words, they would index the power of its continuum. The actual items stored might take the form of suggestive action recipes, improvisational event scripts, or supports that could be used for repriming process. This could include preservation or documentation of the conditioning factors that went into past events (materials, images, sounds, words, concepts, code, media). Their collection would constitute an *archive,* the more multimedia in nature the better. The processual potential they indexed, as it turned over to reanimate the process in new variations, would constitute an *anarchive* (Murphie and SenseLab 2016): an excess-over the archive fueling the continued self-production of the process as an autonomous subjectivity-without-a-subject. The anarchive is a *surplus-value of storage.* Through its anarchiving, the emergent collectivity would grow and prolong itself into a singular *varietal culture.*

Speculative strategy g. Accumulation. There would be no drive to accumulate anything other than techniques of relation and the archival elements fueling the anarchive. The digital platform involved would be open source, freely available for uptake and adaptation. The process seeds would not be proprietary. They would be meant to *disseminate.* This would make the project an open, dissipative system. Although it would tend toward its own continuance, it would not be afraid to die, either by its own potential-crunching volatility going off-kilter or by extreme success (exhausting the pool of potential it was effectively conditioned to mobilize). Even in death, it would live on in the process seeds it disseminated. Self-preservation would not be its aim. This willingness to *risk itself* would safeguard its quality of adventure, and prevent it from becoming an institution: an apparatus of capture driven by a will to systematically reproduce itself, rather than processually spin off qualitatively different versionings of itself, free to go wild. It would dedicate itself to *rewilding, not reproduction*. This is an aspect of the process's anarchic disposition.

Speculative strategy h. Incentivization. There would be no incentivization by promises of quantifiable individual gain. The adventure of the ongoing collective self-improvisation would be its own incentive. The process itself would serve as a qualitative *attractor* for emergent-collectivity production. Attractors orient activity, immanent to a process's self-running, rather than subordinate it to goals or preprogrammed results imposed from without. They operate by purely affective means. They do not goad, discipline, channel, obligate, or obviate. They *lure*. They do not premold or premodel results. They stir up self-driving tendencies predisposed to move in the direction they indicate, their attractive power inflecting them en route into producing variations on themselves. They are leaveners of event-based taking-form. Attractors are lures for the *autonomous self-expression* of creative process. They are echoes of futurity in the present, drawing tendencies out of the past into new adventures. They are an ever-present future-dimension of event-conditioning. They prompt tendencies to outdo themselves (exceed their own slavish repetition).

Speculative strategy i. The digital. The digital merits inclusion on the list of dangers to ward off to the extent that it lends itself to forming social or cultural bubbles fearful of the outside, or embodies a transactionalist exchange model (Strategy j). A digital platform is necessary, of course, to implement a cryptocurrency (T95). But if the digital platform is considered *the* process, rather than a platform of relation through which the process phase-shifts, a closed culture, and the accompanying entropy, can quickly set in. The digital platform would be conceived as a pivot for the process, spinning off creative energies into offline collaborative *events*. The archival action-traces of the events would be returned to the online archive. They would then be dynamized by procedures, both automated and manual, designed to render them anarchival: apt to reactivate as forerunner conditioning factors for events to come. The offline events would be where the surplus-value of life would be most intensely lived. The self-affirming value produced by the process would revolve around the production of embodied surplus-value of event. The digital platform would be the technical engine of the creative process, but not its experiential heart. The relation between the digital platform and the offline events spinning off from it would be *transductive.* By transductive is meant the continuing of a process across phase-shifts moving the process from one qualitatively different differential field of emergence to another, each hosting their own qualitative differentials and manners of taking-form.

Speculative strategy j. Transactional exchange. *Smart contracts* would be used internally for easing into collaboration and communicating the relational ethos of the varietal culture to newcomers. They would not be contracts in the traditional sense, but more like *process movers.* For example, they could be used as gateways that organize a participant's getting to know the process and being welcomed into it. This would avoid the heavy-handed disciplinary gesture of requiring acquiescence to a formal set of rules as a condition of entry (the widely used strategy that is the digital equivalent of the outmoded "social contract" so much a part of liberal democracy). They could also be used to crystallize activity and attention around emergent propositions, and to nudge them over the threshold into an eventful taking-form. In this capacity, they would replace the formal "governance" structures built into blockchain and postblockchain projects, even the most alter-economic in inspiration. There would be no membership, no formal vetting of newcomers, and no structured-in unequal distribution of power (for example, between newcomers and old-timers, even founders). The danger of trolls and willful destroyers would be assumed as a risk of adventure. Again, if the project died for lack of adequate immune response to these threats, its disseminative nature would mean it could always reseed itself elsewhere. It would be designed to be self-grafting, rather than self-preserving and self-reproducing. The fusional process driving it would carry fissile potential.

Speculative strategy k. Decision. There would be *no formal decision-making,* whether consensus-based or voting-based. This would be at the heart of the anarchistic aspect. Consensus-based decision-making has been experimented with for many decades among alternative political and social movements and has been resurgent in recent years in the assembly-based movements coming out of the Arab Spring and Occupy. Conceived as a form of direct democracy, often under the anarchist banner, in practice it easily leads to paralysis: the despotism of the most cantankerous or the least adventurous. Since an individual (or in "consensus-seeking high majority rule" models, a small minority) can block any action, it can lead not to anarchic adventure and effervescence, but to least-common-denominator ennui. This is not so different from the net effect of traditional majority-rule voting, which weeds out exactly the kind of outlier tendencies that an anarchic process needs to fold into its varietal culture and nurture, encouraging them to unfold and carry themselves to their highest power, in self-acting relational autonomy. Voting destroys collective process (except those whose systematic reason for being is the exercise of normative regulatory power). It stages a simulacrum of collectivity, requiring that individuals act utterly alone at the same time. What that yields is not an emergent relational spin-off effect, but a statistical aggregation-effect. This is a use of quanitification procedures that is pronouncedly de-creative. In an anarcho-communist process, decision-making would be truly self-organizing. The positive orienting power of attractors would be used. *Decisions would be lured* into self-organizing. Anyone would be empowered to throw down a lure, in the form of a proposition for a gathering of the collective energies. Any decision resulting would be *affective* and improvisational rather than deliberative and procedural. If the lure fell on fertile ground and succeeded in gathering creative momentum, the proposition would move over the threshold toward actualization. This would require that propositions be offered in the spirit of a gift, without the obligation of payback: *the gift freed from the dialectic of the countergift*. This willingness to offer without a guarantee of return would be the core quality of the processual ethos. It would qualify the process as, fundamentally, a participation-based gift economy. The generosity expected would not be styled as a personal character trait, but as a quality of the collective process moving the individual, and moving through the individual: a *surplus-value of care*. No assumptions would be made about "human nature" and whether it is fundamentally "good" or "evil" by normative standards. Such debates are beside the processual point. The ethical quality of the process would pertain not to the individuals per se, but to the nature of the subjectivity-without-a-subject embodied in the always-emergent collectivity. The process would leverage the *power of the impersonal* (native to the immanent outside). The possibilities for distributed agency offered by interactive digital platforms are key to mobilizing the self-organizing, anarchic potential of surplus-value of care. The mechanism for the self-organizing of decision would hinge on a collective attunement on the part of the participants to the moments when the process is felt to be reaching a threshold where a proposition is ripe to tip over into its actualization in an event. An algorithmic means would have to be found to register the fluctuations in the affective intensity composed by the tendencies in play, in order to make the approach to these tipping points palpable. In other words, a digital *affect-o-meter* registering intensity would have to be invented.

Speculative strategy 1. Humanism. The operationalization of the subjectivity-without-a-subject expressing itself in the iterative taking-form of emergent collectivity would be a processual rebuttal of humanism. Humanism's focus is on the individual (bourgeois) person as the beginning and the end of all that is considered to matter in life. Anarcho-communist process would be transindividual: linking infrapersonal tendencies to superpersonal factors. It would be *more-than-human.* Here also, the digital platform can assist. *Processual operators* (basically, glorified bots) could be used to introduce strategic doses of contingency and whimsy into the interactions. These would be relational, both in the sense that they would be responding to qualitative differentials tendentially churning in the interactions, and in the sense that they would operate as cues or triggers that might modulate the interaction consequent to their intervention in ways that were not anticipatable, thus bringing less accessible potentials into relief. These fabulatory creatures would act as punctual potential-churns, introducing a nonhuman element of play. Their ability to play to creative effect would depend on their being tied to algorithmic analysis running in the background that would be capable of detecting and *indexing creative differentials constituting qualitative tendencies.* This requires effectively turning the tables on quantity, committing quantitatively based (digital) analysis to the mining not of numbers or statistics per se, but of qualitative potentials: a not derivative-unlike convergence between quality and quantity (T46), shorn of the drive to accumulation. The success of the affect-o-meter involved in decision-tipping would depend on this as well. What would be needed is what Nora Bateson has called *"warm data,"* in her call for the development of techniques for harvesting "transcontextual information about the interrelationships that integrate a complex system" (Bateson 2017). The invention and operationalization of warm data is absolutely fundamental to the entire economization project. The process could only create an economy that did not end up resubsuming surplus-value of life under the drive for economic surplus-value if ways are found of indexing qualitative potential by quantitative means without annulling it. The *economization would have to run on affective intensities* affirmed for their own value. When this is achieved, the very nature of measurement will change. Now snaking through the coils of the process, integrated into its most intimate operations, measurement has been *converted into a qualitative conditioning factor,* so dynamically entangled with the creative process as to contribute to *changing the nature of what it measures*: it becomes a dimension of the qualitative becoming running through the creative process engine. This would carry to the limit the convergence financial derivatives tend toward in the name of accumulation, falling short as a result. Existing qualitative analysis tools might be conscripted to the task, to which machine learning might also be adaptable. The economization tools would also have to pivot on suprapersonal and infrapersonal movements, and the differentials between them, rather than centering on inputs, opinions, or tendencies attributable to individual humans. All analysis would have to be carried out in keeping with the transversal modus operandi of the process and the transindividual ethos in-forming it. A critical concern would be to *register the way in which subtendencies have insisted on themselves, even if they were not brought to full expression.* A surplus of anarchival potential is found in the differential between these un-self-accomplished subtendential insistencies and the global emergence-effect they contributed to, if only in the way they ended up being skirted around or thwarted (the way in which they were "negatively prehended," Whitehead would say, recalling that negative prehension "expresses a bond"; 1978, 41). These also-rans constitute a horde of leftover forerunner potentials that can be reactivated to make an eventful difference. They lurk in the process, and can be brought back to bear. Hording, not hoarding.

Speculative strategy m. Privatization. For there to be no accumulation, there would have to be no private ownership within the project. No appropriation. There would be no distribution of individual shares of any kind. Any economic value spun off would be returned to the collective process. This is the communistic aspect.

Speculative strategy n. Purity. The order of the day would be creative duplicity. Purity, and the sense of personal moral superiority that goes along with it, would not be a factor. Since all of this would be happening in a pore of the dominant society, it would be necessary for the project to find ways of processually coupling with the existing economy in order to sustain itself. Even more importantly, it would couple with other alter-economy projects operating along different lines, as well as alternative political movements of all kinds, including the

burgeoning activist peer-to-peer world (https://p2pfoundation
.net). The project would be a collaborative partner in an *ecology
of powers*. Its creative process engine would function as a *driver
of primary resistance* disseminating tendentially postcapitalist
process seeds into its surrounding fields, with which it strives
to enter into mutually beneficial symbiosis, all the while feeding off the dominant capitalist economy where needed, rather
than feeding it, awaiting a tipping point to be reached where
the alter-economic web would be capable of taking over from
capitalism.

T95

The crucial question is: How can a creative process engine that
stays true to its mission of producing surplus-value of life for its
own sake at the same time style itself an economization process capable of interfacing with the dominant economy in self-sustaining
ways? That kind of complicity will be necessary transitionally, as
the postcapitalist pores of the current society take the time they
need to dilate and merge into an alter-world of their own. The only
way this might be possible, if the present analysis holds, would
be by *exploiting the two-sidedness of intensive magnitude*: the way
in which the qualitative and the quantitative embrace each other
without touching, while taking flight together in the caduceus of
intensive magnitude.

FABULATION. Say that algorithmic techniques were found to
index potential. What they would register would be qualitative
differentials preaccelerating emergent tendencies. This would
require a mode of mathematization beyond counting and statistics. The count of tendencies is largely irrelevant for processual purposes, for the simple reason that the potential
in-forming them is supernumerary. To get at this supernumer-
acy of potential, the quantitative analysis involved would have

to bear on *differentials as such*: spreads, contrasts, ratios, frequencies, distributions, vectors converging and diverging, varying distances. The qualitative characters of the items in the online archive (images, sounds, words, etc.) would be analyzed to extract these differentials in ways designed to be indicative of fluctuating relation. This would put the machinic finger on the pulse of the power of the continuum (T78 Schol. b) as it is in-forming a taking-form destined to separate itself out from the flow as an evental drop of processual experience. The aim would be to *register the anarchival movement of surplus-value of life at the emergent level.* One possibility (doubtless there are many) might be that the differentials would be rendered in the form of a topological figure that would fold into new shapes each time the pulse was taken. From the torsions of the figure, vector values could be extracted that would register the fluctuations of the affective intensities coursing through the online interactions over time. This would amount to a derivative measure of process, indexing the flow of creative activity, treated as an intensive magnitude. To ensure that the measurement captures the creative advance, certain passages across thresholds of taking-form could be given special weight: tipping points where a proposition gels, where a proposition passes into offline actualization, and where the action-traces of actualized events are returned to the online platform to further the anarchive. This is where, pragmatically, the two-sidedness of intensive magnitude comes in. Internal to the online platform, the creative process engine would continue as usual, using its suite of relationally oriented smart contracts, processual operators, and other tools, oblivious to the mathematical harvest going on in parallel. The mathematical indexing would parallel the *magmatic* flow of the creative advance. It would render, into a quantifiable expression, the power of its continuum as it peaks and irrupts in discrete relational events of collective experimentation, to continue its turnover across them. From the outside perspective, refracting the quantitative expression that has been extracted from the process back onto it, this "magma" of event-potential could be looked upon differently: it could be thought of as an un-unitized *money mass*. Say there is a *cryptocurrency* associated with the project. The quantifications of the fluctuations of creative potentials taking-form could be used to "mine" units of the currency. A certain number of units of currency would be minted at regular intervals, indexed to the magmatic flow and its irruption into eventful takings-form. Call the cryptocurrency "*Occurrency*" (in keeping with the evental nature of the project). Occurrency would not be used internal to the creative process engine. There would be a digital membrane separating the creative collaborative process from its minting of conventional economic values and, through them, its participation in the larger economic environment. Occurrency would lurk on the outside of the membrane, paralleling the qualitative value-producing process as its quantitative flipside. On this side, the aspect of intensive magnitude that lends itself to quantification would be operative. Internally to the process, it would be the other side of intensive magnitude—where it dips into the playing-out of potential composed by qualitative differentials—that would be operative. The membrane would exist only to manage the two-sidedness of intensive magnitude, operating as an economizing filter. The continuum of magmatic potential would filter through the membrane, appearing for that purpose as a money mass undergoing unitization. The unitization would convert the inside flow of the process into an outside (oc)currency. Outside the membrane, Occurrency would fulfill the threefold function of money. This economization membrane would be the only way in which the creative process engine would be enclosed. In other respects, the process would be radically open—to new participants, to the external world of offline events, and to the immanent outside of creative potential. Occurrency would be liminal in relation to the creative process engine, and interstitial in relation to other alter-economic spaces. The creative process engine would exist in an environment of other alternative "economic spaces," each with their own dedicated cryptocurrencies operating along whatever lines their collective, commons-oriented projects required. Each currency would be convertible into a surrounding currency that would be interoperable with all of them. Call it "*Space.*" The economic spaces would buttress each other: each would contribute a portion of the value they minted to the spaces around it, encouraging cooperation. The environment would be designed for symbiosis rather than competition. To complete the complex open system design of the environment of alter-economic spaces, there might be an underlying cryptocurrency that Space would link with. Call it "*Gravity.*" Gravity would participate in the burgeoning cryptocurrency market, providing an outlet through which the economic spaces cohabiting the alter-economic environment could interface with Bitcoin, other cryptocurrencies, or national currencies, using Space as a transitional medium. This would create the possibility for the Occurrency minted by the creative process engine to be converted to cash value, on an as-needed basis. In this way, the project could provision itself with the goods and services it had no choice but to source from the dominant economy, but which it needed to fuel its self-driving on its own processual terms (travel, food, and accommodation for participants in the offline events, materials, etc.). The resulting economy would be an economy of *abundance,* because its "underlying" would be activity, and the activity, though fluctuating, would be ongoing. It would be the force of its continuing that would be harnessed. The economization would bear on the power of the continuum: a self-renewing *plenum* of subjective becoming, rather than an objective scarcity of resources. It is important to note that the rendering of warm data registering the movements of magmatic potential toward a determinate taking-form (an emergent decision) could be given a double expression. Inside the altereconomic space, on the platform, it could be visualized (or audiovisualized or otherwise figured) to form an affect-o-meter (T94 Strat. k) following the qualitative-relational flow in real time, or in periodic refreshings of the figure. This registering of fluctuations in the affective intensity indexing the playing out of tendencies would be an aesthetic accompaniment to the process, in the process: an immanent accentuation-differentiation of it. In a word, it would be an *affective resonator*. It would co-condition emergent takings-form by making the ebb and flow of the process immediately palpable. This could potentially activate the collective sensing of formative thresholds, and push them over the edge into becoming tipping points (immanent decisions). By this device, the quantification apparatus moving the process outward would converge with the creative advance of the collective qualitative becoming on the inside. The monetization occurring through the passage through the membrane would appear on the outside as the economized tip of the creative iceberg. The process would effectively bifurcate. Crucially, the bifurcation point would be twofold. It would be double-actioned: the unitizing quantification would filter the process out into its monetarization outside the membrane, while at the same time, as a function of the same registering of qualitative differentials, the affect-o-meter as immanent decision-making aid would be folding the process integrally back into itself. The process would be simultaneously *refracted* outward and fed it back into to its own immanent *inflections*, in synchronous oscillation. This would produce a single, two-way movement, on the one side toward a countable expression of magnitude, and on the other back into intensity. The complementary relation between the monetary refraction without and the self-advance of the process taking another creative turn within would be the source of confidence in Occurrency. It would "commensurate" the qualitative production of surplus-value of life that is the continuing life of the process with the monetary surplus-value spun off from it, so that the outside exchange-value of Occurrency both within the ecology of alter-economic spaces and (through Gravity) on the general cryptocurrency market would be perceived as an effective "pricing" of the "underlying asset"—which is, paradoxically, the very project of producing the incommensurable. The overall strategy would be to make the process an *effective paradox* (playing creative duplicity to the hilt).

FACT. The SenseLab (www.senselab.ca) has been working on just such a project since early 2016, in collaboration with the developer of Space and Gravity, the Economic Space Agency (ECSA). The creative-process engine is called the *Three Ecologies Process Seed Bank* (named after the book by Félix Guattari; 2014). The offline events will power an alter-university project called the *Three Ecologies Institute.* Like the SenseLab, the 3E Institute will operate at the intersection of art, philosophy, and activism. Its aim is to evolve collaborative techniques of relation for the collective valorization of forces of primary resistance. Its only product is the process of emergent collectivity. The ideas contained in this manifesto were developed through this project, in dialogue with a network of alter-economic thinkers in and around the Economic Space Agency. The orientation of the concepts, and in many cases their content, has been strongly in-formed by the collective making-thinking process of the SenseLab and would not have been possible without it.

This particular articulation is just one among many churning in the creative cauldron of the ongoing 3E project. It does not represent a consensus (just one proposed suite of attractors) and will undoubtedly change significantly through the evolution of the collective process. Much will depend on whether the speculative adventure of inventing digital techniques for numerically expressing the play of qualitative differentials in the way just described pans out, and on the creation of a functioning affect-o-meter associated with those techniques. Much will also depend on how successful initiatives like ECSA and Holochain (with which the SenseLab is also collaborating exploratorily) prove to be in their speculative adventure of reinventing the blockchain and smart contracts without slipping past creative duplicity toward financial capital into creative process–destroying compromise. The SenseLab is maintaining a certain processual autonomy in relation to specific platforms by prototyping offline analogue versions of all of the qualitative-relational operators that would compose its proposed digital platform. In fact, the digital operators are modeled to begin with on analogue strategies experimented with throughout the SenseLab's fifteen-year history (Manning and Massumi 2014, 83–151). This builds in a margin of play in the form of platform-independence, and militates against code-fundamentalism ("code is law") or techno-utopianism. Crypto-failure could still topologically morph into Three Ecologies success. This is not a technological project; it is a life project.

T96

Although there is no room for purism, given the reality of complicity and the need for creative duplicity, it is crucial, in order to maintain course toward the postcapitalist future, to make room for an *extremist* or maximalist tendency—a *limit-case attractor set* that is not afraid to engage with the processual mutation that is financial capital and grapple with its new technological crypto-avatars, while implementing, in as intense and comprehensive a way as possible, strategies for warding off the unwanted return of market functions, prefiguring to the greatest extent presently possible a postcapitalist future.

SCHOLIUM. The account presented here is intentionally extremist in its insistence on keeping the traditional definition of money and the individualist presuppositions of liberalism and libertarianism out of the heart of the alter-economization process by exploiting the two-sidedness of intensive magnitude. The membrane segregates the unitization/monetization necessary for interfacing with the dominant economy from the mode of operation of the creative-process engine in its own right. This is designed to shelter the purely qualitative economy growing in the tendentially postcapitalist pore of the field of life constituted by the project from creeping capitalist recolonization, while enabling it to indulge in life-sustaining practices of creative duplicity. The maximalist orientation of the present account is not meant to serve as a model. This would return to normative regulation. Rather, it is meant as a lure encouraging alter-economic experimentations to stretch their tending over the capitalist horizon toward vistas that are not yet in view, and can barely as yet be thought possible. Its function is to serve as a *tensor* to the postcapitalist beyond: a kind of *probe-head* to the future-impossible. The whole notion of running an actual economy on affective intensities affirmed purely for their qualitative surplus-value of life may well prove impossible. There is a palpable edge of madness to it. But if the oft-repeated phrase that it is easier to imagine the end of the world than the end of capitalism captures our contemporary condition, then a touch of madness and concerted lure to the impossible is exactly what is needed if the end of the world is to be avoided—and the way we are going, it is looking likely that the end of the world will coincide with the end of capitalism, through capitalism's own madness: its predicating its process on endless growth (which is how it figures the future-impossible that it destructively takes as its lure). The creative process engine envisioned here would not judge or oppose alter-economic spaces negotiating their creative duplicity differently, even in ways that reintroduce certain market features (such as tokens). It would enter into an *ecology of practices* with them. Cohabiting a symbiotic environment with them, it would act, by its very presence in their midst, as an ongoing anarcho-communist *propaganda of the deed*. Neither would it demand purism of the individuals participating in the project. No one would have to be "all in." Straddling economic domains would be the rule. Ecologically speaking, a complex field of intertwined alter-economies of different kinds (sharing economies, gift economies, local currencies, collectivist intentional communities, etc.) would be the most robust. While the various pores grew and combined to form a complex, expanding, prefiguratively postcapitalist field, angles of continued participation in the dominant capitalist economy would likely be a necessity of survival for most participants. The alter-economic approach itself would enter into an ecology of practices with anticapitalist political movements choosing other grounds of action. Movements privileging the micropolitical (Massumi 2015b, 47–82) would be most symbiosis-friendly. Strategic forays into macropolitical interventions—approaches that are demands-oriented rather than prefigurative-process-oriented, and prescriptive/programmatic rather than affective/intensive—would not be shied away from on principle. Most of all, direct-action tactics of refusal, blockage, and breakage would remain an essential ingredient, bolstering and defending movements of primary resistance.

There would be no hard-and-fast principles, no top-down directive strategies. Pragmatism, with a view to the concertation of potentially confluent but irreducibly singular self-affirming movements, would be the order of the day—on the condition that it remained overall a *speculative pragmatism* tensoring toward the invention of a postcapitalist future. Different species of activism and intervention would cohabit an ecology of alter-powers, supported by a growing culture, fertilized by a relational ethos. The ideal: not purity, but creative duplicity, most ecological. Duplicity creatively practiced, not as an end in itself but as an impetus toward its own obsolescence, in approach to a global tipping point: a process-wide "turnaround" point performing the etymological meaning of revolution.

T97

The madness of *basing an actual economy on affective intensities* is not entirely without precedent (and may not be so mad as that).

SCHOLIUM. As discussed earlier, the financial markets, which have taken over the pilot function of the capitalist economy, run more on affect and intensification than on underlying economic "fundamentals" (T11 Schol. a; T46 Schol. b). In a sense, the alter-economic strategies advocated here are taking the most advanced sectors of the neoliberal capitalist economy not at their word (which is ambiguated by lip-service to outmoded classical-liberal economic rhetoric) but at what they do at their furthest processual reach: their own propaganda of the deed. If the financial markets can levitate themselves using affective intensities as the engine of their process, why couldn't another kind of economy similarly bootstrap itself? One that does not just run on affective intensities but affirms them purely for the surplus-value of life they yield. One that refrains from brutally subsuming them under the profit-hungry quantification mechanisms driving capitalist accumulation. One that economizes alter-wise.

T98

If the revaluation of values expresses itself in an aesthetics of value-embodying creative adventure, it has to *embrace beauty*—while *divesting it of its connotations of harmony.*

SCHOLIUM. In the aesthetics of value, beauty would be a pure-quality word for an actualized quantum of value. As value-word, it would displace the profit-word. It would be the abstract figure of surplus-value of life. Adventure is the way beauty outdoes itself, in self-driving processual turnover. Thought of in tandem with the dynamic of adventure, beauty does not privilege the steady-state notion of harmony. Based on a play of qualitative differentials—irreducible contrasts whose tensions activate incommensurable tendencies—this kind of beauty would involve an unabstractable element of *discord* (Whitehead 1967, 257, 259–60, 266, 282–83). Traces of zest, adventure, and wonder troubling its pure quality would keep beauty processually honest. In the processual vitality they make felt, discord would be palpable. *Dissensus*—the unerasability of qualitative differentials and the incommensurability of co-motional tendencies—would be affirmed. A certain off-balancedness would accompany the process. It, also, would be affirmed. This would prevent a systemic self-satisfaction (reproduction) or structural entropy (stasis; anaesthesia) from setting in. Politically, the trick would be to prevent this constitutive imbalance from running the process aground. The process would have to be so conditioned as to *metabolize dissensus,* fusing its co-motion of tendencies into an iterative rhythm of creative advance, integrally expressing itself, in drop after drop of surplus-valued experience. The trick would be to *make incommensurables compossible.* This is precisely what an ecology does.

T99

Speaking processually, as well as ethico-aesthetically, the transition to a postcapitalist future is best achieved *nonviolently.*

SCHOLIUM A. Becoming-reactive is the epitome of ugliness— and violence breeds reaction. Violence is dissensual in a curtailing and destructive way, rather than creatively and metabolically. Discord as a processual virtue associated with beauty is mutually intensifying, not eliminative or limitative. If violence is used, it must first be converted into an affirmative force (Deleuze 1983, 70). The only thing to be eliminated is the becoming-reactive of forces.

SCHOLIUM B. Given the perhaps insurmountable difficulty of employing violence affirmatively, the revaluation of values would remain as *tendentially nonviolent* as possible. That means that nonviolence is practiced not on principle as a personally ascribed-to moral imperative, but pragmatically as a transindividually enacted *processual virtue.*

Bibliography

Ayache, Elie. 2010. *The Blank Swan: The End of Probability*. Chichester, U.K.: Wiley.

Ayache, Elie. 2016. "On Black-Scholes." In *Derivatives and the Wealth of Societies,* ed. Lee and Martin, 240–51. Chicago: University of Chicago Press.

Bataille, Georges. 1988. *The Accursed Share: An Essay on General Economy. Volume 1: Consumption.* Trans. Robert Hurley. New York: Zone Books.

Bateson, Nora. "Warm Data." https://norabateson.wordpress.com/2017/05/28/warm-data/.

Bell, John. 2013. "Continuity and Infinitesimals." *Stanford Encyclopedia of Philosophy.* https://plato.stanford.edu/entries/continuity/.

Beller, Jonathan. 2017. "The Fourth Determination." *e-flux journal* 85 (October). http://www.e-flux.com/journal/85/156818/the-fourth-determination/.

Bergson, Henri. 2001. *Time and Free Will: An Essay on the Immediate Data of Consciousness.* Mineola, N.Y.: Dover.

Bey, Hakim. 2003. *T.A.Z.: The Temporary Autonomous Zone, Ontological Anarchy, and Poetic Terrorism*, 2d edition. New York: Autonomedia.

Bryan, Dick, and Michael Rafferty. 2006. *Capitalism with Derivatives: A Political Economy of Financial Derivatives, Capital, and Class*. London: Palgrave-Macmillan.

Bryan, Dick, and Michael Rafferty. 2007. "Financial Derivatives and the Theory of Money." *Economy & Society* 36, no. 1: 134–58.

Bryan, Dick, and Michael Rafferty. 2013. "Fundamental Value: A Category in Transformation." *Economy & Society* 42, no. 1: 130–53.

Cooper, Melinda. 2008. *Life as Surplus: Biotechnology and Capitalism in the Neoliberal Era*. Seattle: University of Washington Press.

Dean, Kenneth, and Brian Massumi. 1993. *First and Last Emperors: The Body of the Despot and the Absolute State*. New York: Autonomedia.

Deleuze, Gilles. 1983. *Nietzsche and Philosophy*. Trans. Hugh Tomlinson. New York: Columbia University Press.

Deleuze, Gilles. 1988. *Spinoza: Practical Philosophy*. Trans. Robert Hurley. San Francisco: City Lights.

Deleuze, Gilles. 1989. *Cinema 2: The Time-Image*. Trans. Hugh Tomlinson and Robert Galeta. Minneapolis: University of Minnesota Press.

Deleuze, Gilles, and Félix Guattari. 1983. *Anti-Oedipus*. Trans. Robert Hurley, Mark Seem, and Helen R. Lane. Minneapolis: University of Minnesota Press.

Deleuze, Gilles, and Félix Guattari. 1987. *A Thousand Plateaus*. Trans. Brian Massumi. Minneapolis: University of Minnesota Press.

Foucault, Michel. 1994. *The Order of Things: An Archaeology of the Human Sciences*. New York: Vintage.

Foucault, Michel. 2007. *Security, Territory, Population: Lectures at the Collège de France, 1977–1978*. Ed. Michel Senellart. Trans. Graham Burchell. New York: Palgrave Macmillan.

Foucault, Michel. 2008. *The Birth of Biopolitics: Lectures at the Collège de France 1978–1979*. Trans. Graham Burchell. New York: Palgrave Macmillan.

Golumbia, David. 2016. *The Politics of Bitcoin: Software as Right-wing Extremism*. Minneapolis: University of Minnesota Press.

Guattari, Félix. 1995. *Chaosmosis*. Trans. Paul Bains and Julian Pefanis. Bloomington: Indiana University Press.

Guattari, Félix. 2014. *The Three Ecologies*. Trans. Ian Pindar and Paul Sutton. London: Bloomsbury.

Hardt, Michael, and Antonio Negri. 2004. *Multitude: War and Democracy in the Age of Empire*. Cambridge, Mass.: Harvard University Press.

Hardt, Michael, and Antonio Negri. 2009. *Commonwealth*. Cambridge, Mass.: Harvard University Press.

Ingham, Geoffrey. 2004. *The Nature of Money*. Cambridge, U.K.: Polity.

Iaconesi, Salvatore. 2017. "The Financialization of Life." https://startupsventurecapital.com/the-financialization-of-life-a90fe2cb839f.

Keynes, John Maynard. 1973. "The General Theory of Employment." In *The Collected Writings of John Maynard Keynes*, vol. 14, 109–23. London: Macmillan. Originally published 1937.

Kohn, Eduardo. 2013. *How Forests Think: Toward an Anthropology beyond the Human*. Berkeley: University of California Press.

Knorr Cetina, Karen, and Alex Preda. 2007. "The Temporalization of Financial Markets: From Network to Flow." *Theory, Culture & Society* 24, nos. 7–8: 116–38.

Lazzarato, Maurizio. 2012. *The Making of Indebted Man: An Essay on the Neoliberal Condition*. Los Angeles: Semiotext(e).

Lazzarato, Maurizio. 2015. *Governing by Debt*. Los Angeles: Semiotext(e).

Lee, Benjamin, and Randy Martin, eds. 2016. *Derivatives and the Wealth of Societies*. Chicago: University of Chicago Press.

Manning, Erin. 2009. *Relationscapes: Movement, Art, Philosophy*. Cambridge, Mass.: MIT Press.

Manning, Erin. 2016. *The Minor Gesture*. Durham, N.C.: Duke University Press.

Manning, Erin. Forthcoming. "Experimenting Immediation— Collaboration and the Politics of Fabulation." *Immediations*. Ed. Erin Manning, Anna Munster, and Bodil Marie Stavning Thomsen. London: Open Humanities Press.

Manning, Erin, Bodil Marie Stavning Thomsen, and Anna Munster. Forthcoming. *Immediations*. London: Open Humanities Press.

Manning, Erin, and Brian Massumi. 2014. *Thought in the Act: Passages in the Ecology of Experience*. Minneapolis: University of Minnesota Press.

Martin, Randy. 2015. *Knowledge LTD: Toward a Social Logic of the Derivative*. Philadelphia: Temple University Press.

Marx, Karl. 1976. *Capital: A Critique of Political Economy, Volume 1*. Trans. Ben Fowkes. London: Penguin.

Marx, Karl. 1991. *Capital: A Critique of Political Economy, Volume 3*. Trans. David Fernbach. London: Penguin.

Marx, Karl. 1993. *Grundrisse: Foundations for a Critique of Political Economy (Rough Draft)*. Trans. Martin Nicolaus. London: Penguin.

Massumi, Brian. 2014a. "Envisioning the Virtual." In *The Oxford Handbook of Virtuality*, ed. Mark Grimshaw, 55–70. Oxford: Oxford University Press.

Massumi, Brian. 2014b. *The Power at the End of the Economy*. Durham, N.C.: Duke University Press.

Massumi, Brian. 2014c. *What Animals Teach Us about Politics*. Durham, N.C.: Duke University Press.

Massumi, Brian. 2015a. *Ontopower: War, Powers, and the State of Perception*. Durham, N.C.: Duke University Press.

Massumi, Brian. 2015b. *Politics of Affect*. London: Polity.

Massumi, Brian. 2017a. *The Principle of Unrest*. London: Open Humanities Press.

Massumi, Brian. 2017b. "Virtual Ecology and the Question of Value." In *General Ecology: The New Ecological Paradigm*, ed. Erich Hörl, 345–73. London: Bloomsbury.

Minsky, Hyman P. 1982. "The Financial Instability Hypothesis: Capitalist Processes and the Behavior of the Economy." Hyman P. Minsky Archive. Paper 282. http://digitalcommons .bard.edu/hm_archive/282.

Murphie, Andrew, and the SenseLab. 2016. *The Go-To How-To Book of Anarchiving*. Self-published.

Negri, Antonio. 1996. "Twenty Theses on Marx." In *Marxism beyond Marxism*, ed. Saree Makdisi, Cesare Casarino, and Rebecca E. Karl, 149–80. London: Routledge.

Nietzsche, Friedrich. 2003. *Writings from the Late Notebooks*. Ed. Rüdiger Bittner. Trans. Kate Sturge. Cambridge: Cambridge University Press.

Picketty, Thomas. 2014, *Capital in the Twenty-First Century*. Cambridge, Mass.: Harvard University Press.

Reid, Roddey. 2017. *Confronting Political Intimidation and Public Bullying: A Citizen's Handbook for the Trump Era and Beyond*. Independently published.

Sassen, Saskia. 2017. "Predatory Formations Dressed in Wall Street Suits and Algorithmic Math." *Science, Technology & Society* 22, no. 1: 1–15.

Schmitt, Bernard. 1980. *Monnaie, salaires, et profit*. Albeuve, Switzerland: Castella.

Schultz, Theodore W. 1971. *Investment in Human Capital: The Role of Education and of Research*. New York: Free Press.

Simmel, Georg. 1978. *The Philosophy of Money*. Trans. Tom Bottomore and David Frisby. London: Routledge.

Thaler, Richard H., and Cass Sunstein. 2009. *Nudge: Improving Decisions about Health, Wealth, and Happiness*. London: Penguin.

Viveiros de Castro, Eduardo. 2014. *Cannibal Metaphysics*. Trans. Peter Skafish. Minneapolis: Univocal.

Whitehead, Alfred North. 1967. *Adventures of Ideas*. New York: Free Press.

Whitehead, Alfred North. 1978. *Process and Reality*. New York: Free Press.

BRIAN MASSUMI writes across philosophy, political theory, and art theory. He is author of *Architectures of the Unseen: Essays in the Occurrent Arts* (Minnesota, 2019), editor of *The Politics of Everyday Fear* (Minnesota, 1993), and coauthor, with Erin Manning, of *Thought in the Act* (Minnesota, 2014).